P9-DUV-427

Winterthur's Culinary Collection

Compiled by
Anne Beckley Coleman

A Sampler of Fine American Cooking

The Henry Francis du Pont Winterthur Museum

© 1983 by The Henry Francis du Pont Winterthur Museum, Inc.
All Rights Reserved.
Published 1989 in association with Galison Books.

Designer: Cheryl K. Gibbs
Photography coordinator: Elizabeth Tufts Brown

Profits from this publication go toward
Winterthur's general operating fund.

Fifth Edition
Special thanks to the many members of the Winterthur community
who contributed and tested recipes and without whom
this cookbook would not have been possible.

Library of Congress Catalog Card Number 83-50805

Cover: Herbs and spices were important to the eighteenth-century housewife. She used them to flavor stews, to make sweet-smelling potpourri, and to distill medicines.

Almost every household had a flower garden near the parlor windows and an herb garden by the kitchen door. Plots were laid out in geometric patterns, divided by walks of gravel or crushed shells. The beds were built up from the ground and lined with planks to prevent the soil from washing away.

A housewife dried herbs from her garden by hanging them above a fireplace. Throughout the year, she used herbs in recipes for both food and medicine. Some of the most common herbs grown in the eighteenth century were thyme, rosemary, marjoram, and mint; precious spices had to be imported. The herbs and spices shown here include bay leaves, cloves, peppercorns, cinnamon, and nutmeg. Also shown are an ivory mortar and pestle made in Europe, 1700-1800, and horn shakers, or sanders, made in England or America, 1700-1800.

ISBN 0-912724-14-5

Printed in Korea.

CONTENTS

FOREWORD

Winterthur Museum and Gardens in Delaware is known worldwide as the extraordinary legacy of Henry Francis du Pont (1880-1969). Winterthur is both an art museum and a history museum with a matchless collection of antiques and decorative arts objects made or used in America between 1640-1860. The 89,000 objects are displayed in a nine-story building housing 196 period settings and exhibition areas. Winterthur is also a garden of great scenic beauty that contains many collections of rare plants, flowers and trees in 200 landscaped acres. Finally, Winterthur has a renowned collection of books and manuscripts in its library used by scholars and the general public from all over the world. Indeed, Winterthur is a collection of collections.

Now I invite you to enjoy yet another collection—***Winterthur's Culinary Collection.*** Presented here are treasured recipes gathered from many people associated with Winterthur—Trustees, Friends of Winterthur, members of the Winterthur Guild, guides and staff members, Winterthur Wives, and the du Pont family. Recipes once served at Winterthur are indicated by a **WM.** The reminiscences of Mr. du Pont's daughters, Pauline Harrison and Ruth Lord, also offer a fascinating glimpse into life at Winterthur before it became a museum. We are also indebted to Chef Hubert Winkler and his staff of the Hotel du Pont in Wilmington, Delaware, who have incorporated the recipes published in this volume into menus for special occasions. In a special way, this cookbook is another means for Winterthur to share its knowledge not only of early American life but also of traditional and contemporary American home life and cookery.

Over 50,000 copies of ***Winterthur's Culinary Collection*** have been sold and it is now in a fifth printing. The cookbook has been produced by our marketing division, but its publication is a credit to all of those people who love Winterthur and who have worked toward the successful completion of this project. The photographs and line drawings are of particular interest because they illustrate many objects from the museum's collections. This book is yet another link in Winterthur's expanded program of commercial activity designed to help Winterthur maintain the quality of its educational programs.

After you have enjoyed this collection, I hope you will visit Winterthur so that we may share with you the diversity of our other collections.

Thomas A. Graves Jr.

Thomas A. Graves, Jr.
Director

The Du Pont Dining Room was the family dining room of Mr. and Mrs. Henry Francis du Pont when Winterthur was their home. It is furnished with federal period pieces, including the great mahogany dining table inlaid with an American eagle, made in Baltimore, 1790-1800. Twelve of the mahogany side chairs were made for Victor Marie du Pont when he was attaché to the French Legation in New York between 1795 and 1815. Also exhibited in the room: Benjamin West's unfinished *American Commissioners of the Preliminary Peace Negotiations with Great Britain,* painted ca. 1783; a matched set of six silver tankards made by Paul Revere in Boston; and a collection of Chinese export porcelain.

Shown on the table: a Wedgwood creamware dinner service with hand-painted enamel borders, made in England, 1771-1810; green cut-glass stemware made in England, 1850-70; silver forks in the King's pattern by various New York makers, 1806-45; steel-plated knives in early George III style, probably made in England; ovoid silver dishes made by S. Kirk & Son, Baltimore, ca. 1898; a silver bell made in the United States, 1750-1850; and green and white linens once used in the home of Henry Francis du Pont. The glass and silver-plated plateau in the center has three interlocking pieces supported by eight paw and shell feet; it was made in England, 1795-1815. The cut-glass candelabra were made in England or Ireland, 1790-1800.

REMINISCENCE

When we were children, Winterthur was a working farm with beef and dairy cattle, pigs and sheep, chickens and turkeys, guinea hens, ducks, and pigeons. Consequently, our family and others on the place ate the livestock raised there. We all ate heart, liver, sweetbreads, and tongue as a matter of course. Mother was especially fond of tripe and Father of pigs' feet, and to this day we still like them. The vegetable gardens yielded every imaginable vegetable including an experimental variety each year. One of the latter, which we thought tasted faintly like skunk, did not appear again! We were also given beet tops which we as children disliked but which the grown-ups were fond of saying "tasted as good as spinach."

Our parents observed the French custom of serving many separate courses. Lunch began with an egg dish, in summer often preceded by melon, papaya, or mango. This was sometimes followed by a single vegetable such as asparagus, miniature corn on the cob, or string beans. Next came meat with another vegetable, then salad and dessert. At dinner, soup was the first course followed by fish, meat, and two vegetables (almost never potatoes), then salad, cheese, and finally something sweet. All the food was prepared simply, and usually served without sauce other than natural juices, although currant or mint jelly accompanied certain meats. Our family liked beef and lamb very rare and wild duck scarcely cooked at all. Often these meats had to be returned to the oven for the benefit of those who did not share this taste.

On Christmas night, there was a suckling pig crisply roasted with an apple in its mouth, which followed stew of diamondback terrapin, a kind of turtle which crawled around in our cellar before being dispatched. The terrapins, served in the Baltimore style as distinct from the richer Philadelphia recipe which called for cream sauce, were cooked in their own juices. Among the wineglasses, a glass of sherry was provided at each place to be added to the turtle stew as desired. Another Christmas dish was a large roast turkey with chestnut stuffing surrounded by homemade sausage. This tasted even better than the Thanksgiving turkey, probably because of Christmas stockings and the piney smell of the Christmas tree.

Continued

At any time of year, our dining room table looked beautiful, with different sets of china, place mats, and flower arrangements at both lunch and dinner every day of the week. After dark, the room was lighted by candles, with candlesticks on the table and candelbra standing on the floor. Our family had a remarkable staff including a cook and her assistants, a butler, and two footmen. Father took great pleasure in planning and organizing. He and Mother would consult with each other at length, as well as with the head cook.and the butler, about the meals, but the final decisions as to the table settings and flowers were his alone.

We should point out that Mother much appreciated this arrangement. She was a perfect complement to her husband and as hostess sensed with warmth and skill which individuals would like talking to one another, and seated the table accordingly. White porcelain place cards were used if eight or more people were to be present. These matched Father's white porcelain menu holder, which was helpful in letting us know in advance what favorite dish to save up for.

As children, we were permitted to admire all this, but strict manners were the rule and we were expected to behave as adults from our earliest days. Our mother and father, especially the latter, loved to entertain, and there were many guests at every meal and laughter and lively conversation.

Friends come to Winterthur now in a different way: to see a museum with a superb collection of American decorative arts, surrounded by beautiful woodland gardens, meadows, streams, and hills.

We hope that this cookbook will please both old friends and new ones, following a family tradition at Winterthur that good eating and hospitality are in themselves a form of decorative art.

Pauline du Pont Harrison and Ruth du Pont Lord

Special Occasion Menus

Chef Hubert Winkler of the Hotel du Pont in Wilmington, Delaware, compiled the special occasion menus in the following section using recipes found throughout the cookbook. Foods from the Summer Garden Party menu are shown on the reverse being served buffet style on the terrace of the Winterthur Gallery.

Rear (left to right): Peruvian Potato Salad served in a scalloped pearlware bowl made in Staffordshire, England, 1770-1800; Winterthur Iced Tea in a three-mold glass pitcher, made in the United States, 1825-40; Adonna's Greek Meatballs in an earthenware compote made in Staffordshire, England by Josiah Wedgwood, ca. 1780; glass punch bowl, made in Sandwich, Massachusetts, 1825-35; Marinated Artichoke Hearts in an oval bowl of cut lead glass, made in England, 1790-1802; Party Biscuits in a pearlware basket on tray, made by Shorthose & Company in Staffordshire, England, ca. 1817.

Front (left to right): three-mold glass tumblers and mug, made in the United States, 1820-50; Coffee Cake on a green-glazed earthenware plate, made in Staffordshire, England, 1700-1800; Beach Slaw served in a pearlware bowl made in Staffordshire, England, 1813-30; earthenware castors made in England, 1790-1840; Chicken Dijon on a feather-edged earthenware platter, made in England, 1800-1840.

ELEGANT DINNER FOR SIX

Winterthur Punch

Kennett Square Mushrooms

Cream Of Wild Rice Soup

Crab And Shrimp Soufflé

Boeuf Bourbon

Max's Spinach Salad With Garlic Vinaigrette

Raspberry Mousse

Coffee Royale

SUMMER GARDEN PARTY

Chicken Dijon

Adonna's Greek Meatballs

Marinated Artichoke Hearts — Peruvian Potato Salad

Beach Slaw

Party Biscuits With Smoked Ham

Coffee Cake

Mint Julip — Winterthur Iced Tea

POINT TO POINT RACE TAILGATE PICNIC

Winterthur Punch

Cucumber Soup

Herb Bread — Fruited Iced Tea

Lemon Chicken Breasts

Marinated Vegetable Salad

Oranges in Wine Sauce

BRUNCH BEFORE THE FAIR

Assorted Fresh Fruit

Sausage Strata

David Eyre's Pancakes

Kolaches

SUMMER LUNCHEON ON THE TERRACE

London Broil Stuffed With Mushrooms & Cheese

Spinach And Fruit Salad — Beer Bread

Orange Cake

Fruited Iced Tea

AFTERNOON TEA AT THE CORBIT-SHARP HOUSE

Hot Tea

Double Chocolate Charlotte

Coconut Pound Cake

Georgia Peach Pie

COCKTAILS BEFORE THE OPERA

Wagner's Fish House Punch

Orange Punch

Crab and Cheese Spread With Assorted Crackers

Marinated Mushrooms

Shrimp Gougere

Russian Peasant Dip With Assorted Vegetables

AFTER THEATRE SUPPER

Salmon Spread With Assorted Fancy Crackers

Sassy Chicken — Confetti Rice Salad

Cherries Jubilee

Brandy Coffee Supreme

YULETIDE REVELS

Delaware Crab Puffs

Cream Of Mushroom Soup

Cornish Game Hens With Cranberry Stuffing

Fresh Broccoli Salad

Plum Pudding With Christmas Pudding Sauce

Special Eggnog

Wassail Bowl Punch

TWELFTH NIGHT GALA SUPPER

Sherried Mushroom Consommé

Fillet De Sole Veronique

Stuffed Crown Roast Of Pork

Spinach-Sesame Salad

Parfait Au Grand Marnier

Christmas Punch

During the federal period, from the end of the Revolution through the first quarter of the nineteenth century, enthusiasm for classical taste pervaded all aspects of American life. The "antique style," inspired by new discoveries at Pompeii and Herculaneum, was adopted by citizens of the new nation, who spiritually associated themselves with the Romans. Americans emulated the ancients' qualities of justice, patriotism, liberty, and industry.

The federal style is epitomized by fine proportions and delicate details. Although furniture of the federal period was at first imported to America, American cabinetmakers soon designed and fashioned their own pieces by consulting English pattern books by Hepplewhite, Sheraton, and others. The furniture had graceful outlines and smooth surfaces embellished with wood inlay, inset glass, or painted panels. The wealth of ornament included classical motifs such as the urn, Greek key border, fluting and swags of drapery, and patriotic motifs such as the American eagle, shield, and stars.

Furniture for dining rooms was especially popular during the federal period. Cabinet-makers met the demand for furniture intended to display fine china and silver by developing the china cabinet and the sideboard. The marble-topped mahogany side-board with light inlay and curvilinear backboard shown here was made between 1795 and 1805 by Abner Toppan of Newburyport, Massachussetts, and is a convenient serving place for hors d'oeuvres. A Cheese Ball and Stuffed Mushrooms are both served on silver salvers. The salver with claw and ball feet was made between 1754 and 1774 by Bancroft Woodcock of Wilmington, Delaware; the other with pad feet and gadrooned molding was made between 1754 and 1785 by William Hollingshead of Philadelphia.

Also displayed on the sideboard: a decanter with cut and engraved flutes, sunbursts, and swags, probably made in Germany, 1780-1810; wine glasses with cut patterns, made in England, 1810-30; a silver butter knife made by Shepherd and Boyd of Albany, New York, 1810-20; silver castors made by Benjamin Burt of Boston, Massachussetts, 1750-75; Chinese export porcelain plates with Greek key border, 1810-30; and a porcelain urn with green and gilt decoration made in China, 1780-1800. "The Battle of Lake Erie" was painted ca. 1818, by Louis Garneray of France.

JEZEBEL

Yield: 1 quart
Preparation: 10 minutes

Combine all ingredients by hand. Use as spread for ham, cream cheese, boiled shrimp, egg rolls, or crackers.

1 18-ounce jar apple jelly
1 18-ounce jar pineapple preserves
1½ tablespoons coarsely ground black pepper
1 5-ounce jar horseradish
1 small can (1.2 ounces) dry mustard

Mrs. James Morton Smith

DELAWARE CRAB PUFFS

Serves: 6-8
Preparation: 30 minutes
Cooking: 20-30 minutes
Freeze: Yes

Heat cooking oil to 375°. Mix dry ingredients. In separate bowl, beat the egg and add milk and crab meat. Stir into flour mixture. Mix well. Drop mixture from spoon into hot oil, and fry until delicately browned.

Cooking oil
2 cups flour
3 teaspoons baking powder
½ teaspoon salt
1 egg
1 cup milk
½ pound crab meat

"These are delicious for starters, snacks, or light lunch."
    Mrs. Robert S. Chapin

MUSHROOM SANDWICHES

Yield: 84 sandwiches
Preparation: 20 minutes
Cooking: 20 minutes

Sauté mushrooms in butter for about 5 minutes until liquid from mushrooms evaporates. Drain and cool. Mix in mayonnaise to form a paste. Season with salt, pepper, and cayenne. Remove crusts from 42 slices of bread (reserve remaining bread for other use). Roll bread thin with rolling pin. Spread one side of each slice with additional mayonnaise. Place a heaping teaspoon of filling on long edge of bread and roll up. Cut each roll into 2 pieces on a diagonal. Toast at 400° for 10 to 15 minutes, until bread browns.

1 pound mushrooms, finely chopped
1 tablespoon butter
1 tablespoon mayonnaise, plus additional mayonnaise to spread on bread
Salt and pepper to taste
¼ teaspoon cayenne, or to taste
2 loaves thinly sliced white bread

Virginia Wier

HOT ZUCCHINI PUFFS

Yield: 50 puffs
Preparation: 15 minutes
Baking: 12 minutes

Mix together shredded zucchini and salt, let sit 1 hour, then place in a linen dish towel and squeeze dry. Mix all other ingredients together and stir in zucchini. Spread mixture thickly, about ¼-inch to 1/3-inch high, on toasted bread rounds. Bake at 375° for 12 minutes until lightly browned. Half of recipe works well as a baked topping for an open-faced luncheon sandwich.

2 cups shredded raw, unpeeled zucchini
1 teaspoon salt
½ cup grated Romano or Parmesan cheese
1 cup mayonnaise
1 clove garlic, mashed
4 scallions, minced
1 teaspoon Worcestershire sauce
¼ teaspoon Tabasco sauce
Toasted bread rounds

Mrs. A. Atwater Kent, Jr.

SMOKED TURKEY PATE

Serves: 12
Preparation: 20 minutes (plus 3-4 hours refrigeration)

Sauté onions in butter over low to medium heat until golden brown. Place all ingredients (except vegetables) in blender or food processor; process until smooth. Transfer to bowl. Chill in refrigerator 3 to 4 hours until firm. Serve with vegetables.

1½ tablespoons butter or margarine
¾ cup chopped onion
1½ cup cottage cheese
1/3 pound smoked turkey (or chicken), sliced
¾ cup unchopped parsley
½ tablespoon tarragon
2 tablespoons white vinegar
1 package chicken broth
Pepper
Raw vegetables. Select for color as well as preference: asparagus, broccoli, cauliflower, celery, cucumber, green peppers, sweet red peppers, mushrooms, radishes, zucchini.

"Delicious, quickly prepared, and has eye appeal when arranged with vegetables and disappears quickly."
    Anne C. Herndon

HOT DRIED BEEF DIP

Serves: 12
Preparation: 30 minutes
Baking: 20 minutes
Freeze: Yes
Microwave: Yes

Blend cream cheese with milk. Add all other ingredients, mixing well. Bake at 350° in a 9-inch buttered baking dish for 20 minutes. Serve in baking dish or remove to chafing dish. Serve with crackers for a starter or bagels for brunch.

8 ounces cream cheese, softened
2 tablespoons milk
1 cup sour cream
2 tablespoons chopped onions
2 tablespoons chopped green pepper
¾ cup (8 ounce package) chopped dried beef

Carol Jeanne Gaumer

RUM SAUSAGES

Yield: 48 pieces (recipe may be doubled or tripled)
Preparation: 30 minutes
Baking: 1 hour
Freeze: Yes
Microwave: Yes

Bake or fry sausages until well done. Drain and cool. Cut each sausage into three pieces. Set aside. Place sugar, teriyaki, and rum into saucepan. Cook until sugar has dissolved and syrup comes to boil. Remove from heat. Place sausages and syrup into ovenproof dish. Bake uncovered at 325° for 25 minutes. Drain and serve hot with toothpicks, or serve with syrup in a chafing dish. Reserve syrup to store any leftovers. These keep in refrigerator two weeks. Reheat to serve.

1 pound link sausages (regular size)
½ cup dark brown sugar
½ cup teriyaki sauce
½ cup dark rum

Ellen Virden White

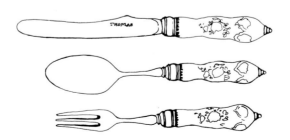

Steel knife, fork and spoon with porcelain handles, 1750-80

AFTERNOON DELIGHT

Serves: 35
Preparation: 10 minutes (plus refrigeration)
Freeze: Yes

Let cream cheese, butter, and sour cream come to room temperature. Cream well and add sugar. Soften envelope of gelatin in ¼ cup cold water. Dissolve over hot water. Add to cream cheese mixture, then add raisins, slivered almonds, and lemon rind. Put in 1 quart mold. Refrigerate. Unmold. May be frozen at this point. When ready to use, thaw. Use mint or watercress and strawberries or cherries as garniture. Serve with saltine crackers.

12 ounces cream cheese
¼ cup butter
½ cup sour cream
½ cup sugar
1 envelope plain gelatin
¼ cup cold water
½ cup white raisins, plumped
1 cup slivered almonds
2 lemon rinds, grated
Saltine crackers

"A special treat with afternoon tea or sherry."
  Janet M. Lemons

SMOKED SALMON SPREAD

Serves: 10-12
Preparation: 12 minutes

In a food processor fitted with a steel blade, mix cheese until well softened and smooth. Add salmon and process until salmon is entirely mixed into cheese. Add lemon juice, Tabasco sauce, and dill weed and process until just mixed. Mound on a plate and surround with light and dark rye bread rounds.

8 ounces cream cheese
¼ pound Nova Scotia salmon
Juice of ½ lemon
Dash Tabasco sauce
1 tablespoon dill weed
Light and dark rye bread rounds

Louise Sloane

CUCUMBER CHEESE BALL

Serves: 30
Preparation: 30 minutes

Peel and chop cucumber. Combine softened cream cheese, cucumber, and garlic salt. Form mixture into mound on serving plate. Cut tomato into 6 wedges. Remove inside part of tomato. Garnish cheese ball with tomato slices wedged vertically into sides of ball. Top center with parsley. Serve with crackers.

1 cup chopped cucumber
16 ounces cream cheese
1 teaspoon garlic salt
1 large tomato
Fresh parsley

Alberta Melloy

KENNETT SQUARE MUSHROOMS

Yield: 20-25 mushrooms
Preparation: 20 minutes
Baking: 20 minutes

Select mushrooms with closed caps. Pull stems from mushrooms and chop finely. Melt butter in skillet and add stems and onion. Sauté until tender and translucent. Stir in remaining ingredients except water. If preferred, parsley may be sprinkled on top instead of mixed in with other ingredients. Fill mushroom caps with mixture, mounding over top. Arrange mushrooms in ovenproof serving dish. At this point mushrooms can be refrigerated up to 24 hours. Before serving, add 2 tablespoons of water to dish. Bake at 350° for 20 minutes. Serve hot.

20-25 fresh medium-sized mushrooms, approximately ½ pound
2 tablespoons butter
1 small onion, minced
1 tablespoon Worcestershire sauce
1/3 cup soft, fine bread crumbs
½ cup shredded sharp Cheddar cheese
Salt and pepper to taste
Parsley
2 tablespoons water

Elizabeth Tufts Brown

CHEESE STUFFED MUSHROOMS

Preparation: 20 minutes
Cooking: 3-5 minutes

Clean the mushrooms and remove the stems. Set aside. Blend together the cream cheese, Parmesan cheese, garlic powder, and Tabasco sauce. Add milk if the mixture is too hard to stir. Stuff the mushrooms and place under the broiler until lightly browned, about 3 to 5 minutes. Serve hot. Mushrooms may be stuffed earlier in the day to be used, refrigerated, and then broiled just before serving.

1 pound fresh mushrooms
8 ounces cream cheese
½ cup grated Parmesan cheese
½ teaspoon garlic powder (or to taste)
Dash Tabasco sauce
1 tablespoon milk (optional)

Lenore K. Holt

Delftware chinoiserie tile, c. 1780

RUSSIAN PEASANT DIP

Serves: 6
Preparation: 5 minutes
(plus 3 hours refrigeration)

Mix all ingredients and chill for 3 hours. Serve in hollowed-out loaf of rye bread, if desired. Sprinkle with paprika. Serve with vegetables.

1 1/3 cup mayonnaise
1 1/3 cup sour cream
2 tablespoons onion flakes
2 tablespoons parsley flakes
2 teaspoons beau monde
2 teaspoons dill weed
12 black olives, chopped fine
Paprika
Assorted vegetables

Orlene Hart

CURRIED COCKTAIL SPREAD

Serves: 12 or more
Preparation: 30 minutes
Cooking: 15 minutes

Sauté onion and celery in butter. Sprinkle with curry powder, stirring 1 minute. Soak gelatin in ¼ cup of chicken broth and heat remaining broth to boiling. Add softened gelatin to boiling broth and stir into curry mixture. Cool and chill mixture until it begins to thicken. Blend in mayonnaise, eggs, and parsley. Pour mixture into a cold, wet mold and chill for 24 hours. Unmold and serve with crackers or pumpernickel bread.

½ medium onion, finely chopped
1 rib of celery, finely chopped
1½ tablespoons butter
2-3 teaspoons curry powder
5 teaspoons unflavored gelatin
2¼ cups chicken broth
1 cup mayonnaise
4 hard-boiled eggs, chopped
2 tablespoons chopped parsley

Lela E. Lippert

PARTY APPLE DIP

Preparation: 10 minutes

Combine liqueur with cream cheese and chill. Serve with apple slices.

¼ cup almond-flavored liqueur
8 ounces cream cheese, softened
Apple slices

Margaret Coveney

CHILI CON QUESO CHEESE SPREAD

Preparation: 15 minutes

Fry bacon and discard all but 2 tablespoons fat; add the remaining ingredients, stirring over low heat until all is melted and blended. Serve hot or cold as a cocktail spread with crackers. Keeps well refrigerated.

5 strips bacon, diced and fried
1 medium onion, chopped
1 green pepper, diced
½ teaspoon crushed red hot peppers
½ teaspoon oregano
½ teaspoon fennel seed
2 cans whole tomatoes, drained and chopped
1/3 pound sharp cheese, cut into chunks
2/3 pound Velveeta cheese, cut into chunks

Karla Stuck Tobar

CHESTERTOWN CRAB SPREAD

Serves: 15-20
Preparation: 30 minutes

Heat soup just to boiling and remove from heat. Dissolve gelatin in boiling water, add to soup, and allow mixture to cool. Beat softened cream cheese and add to cooled soup mixture. Add remaining ingredients. Pour into a buttered 6-cup decorative mold and chill overnight. Unmold onto a bed of lettuce and serve with a variety of crackers.

1 can tomato soup
1 envelope unflavored gelatin
¼ cup boiling water
8 ounces cream cheese, softened
¾ cup mayonnaise
½ cup chopped onions
½ cup chopped celery
Dash of Worcestershire sauce
6½ ounces white crab meat
Lettuce

Darleen Galitsky

Silver coffeepot made by Jacob Hurd, c. 1750

SHRIMP GOUGERE

Serves: 8-10
Preparation: 45 minutes (plus 6 hours refrigeration)
Cooking: 1 hour, 15 minutes

DOUGH:

Heat milk and ¼ cup butter to a boil. Remove from heat and stir in flour, beating until smooth and forming a ball (1 or 2 minutes). Add eggs one at a time, beating briskly after each addition. Stir in Cheddar cheese, mustard, salt, and pepper and cook over low flame, stirring until cheese melts. Shape dough into a ring in a buttered 10-inch pie plate, leaving center empty. Stuff center with plastic wrap to hold shape. Brush dough with egg white. Cover and refrigerate six hours or overnight.

FILLING:

In a large saucepan, bring to boil wine, water, onion, celery, bay leaf, lemon, peppercorns, clove, and one teaspoon salt. Reduce heat and simmer for 5 minutes. Stir in shrimp, return to a boil, then reduce heat and simmer for 4 minutes until shrimp are cooked. Remove shrimp with slotted spoon and reserve. Bring court bouillon back to boil and simmer uncovered for 15 to 20 minutes or until it reduces to ½ cup. Strain. Sauté minced onion in 6 tablespoons butter until wilted. Reduce heat and stir in flour, making a roux. Add court bouillon and simmer, stirring constantly until thick and smooth, about 5 minutes. Stir in chutney, pepper, and reserved shrimp. Remove plastic wrap from pie plate and fill with shrimp mixture. Sprinkle with Parmesan cheese and bake at 400° for 40 to 45 minutes until puffed and brown. Serve immediately. May be made well in advance of serving, then baked at the last minute.

Annie Jones

DOUGH:

1 cup milk
¼ cup butter
1 cup sifted flour
4 eggs
1 cup diced sharp Cheddar cheese
1 teaspoon Dijon-style mustard
½ teaspoon salt
½ teaspoon pepper

FILLING:

1 cup dry white wine
1 egg white, slightly beaten
4 cups water
1 small onion, quartered
½ rib of celery
1 bay leaf
½ lemon, peeled and sliced
6 peppercorns
1 clove
1 teaspoon salt
2 pounds small shrimp, shelled and deveined
½ cup minced onion
6 tablespoons butter
3 tablespoons flour
1/3 cup chopped mango chutney
¼ teaspoon pepper
¼ cup grated Parmesan cheese

Steel flesh fork with brass inlay, 1776

CHEESE-BACON CANAPES

Yield: 70-80 pieces
Preparation: 30 minutes
Baking: 10 minutes
Freeze: Yes

Trim the crusts off bread and cut slices into quarters. Brown the almonds in the butter. Mix all ingredients, except bread squares, in a large bowl. Place small spoonful of mixture on each bread square, place on a cookie sheet and bake at 400° for 10 minutes. Can be frozen on cookie sheet and then stored in a large plastic bag.

1 loaf thin-sliced bread
1 package slivered almonds
1 tablespoon butter
½ pound sharp cheese, grated
8 slices bacon, fried and crumbled
1 small onion, grated
¾ to 1 cup mayonnaise
2½ teaspoons Worcestershire sauce

Norma Adams

DANISH MEATBALLS IN DILL SAUCE

Yield: 80-85 meatballs
Baking: 20-25 minutes

MEATBALLS:
In a large bowl, combine beef, veal or pork, salt, pepper, egg, onion, half-and-half, bread crumbs, allspice, and dill weed. Shape into 1-inch balls; arrange on a rack in a broiler pan. Bake at 375° for 20 to 25 minutes or until browned. Drain cooked meatballs and serve hot with Dill Sauce.

MEATBALLS:
1 pound lean ground beef
½ pound ground veal or lean ground pork
1 teaspoon salt
⅛ teaspoon pepper
1 egg, slightly beaten
1 tablespoon grated onion
¼ cup half-and-half
½ cup soft bread crumbs
⅛ teaspoon ground allspice
2 teaspoons fresh dill weed

DILL SAUCE:
In a small saucepan, melt butter; stir in flour. Stir in broth, salt, and dill weed. Cook and stir over medium heat until thickened. Remove from heat; stir in sour cream.

DILL SAUCE:
¼ cup butter
¼ cup flour
2 cups chicken broth
¼ teaspoon salt
2 teaspoons dried dill weed
1 cup sour cream

Beverley Brainard Fleming

CAVIAR MOUSSE

Serves: 6
Preparation: 15 minutes (plus refrigeration overnight)

Blend the eggs with the butter in food processor, or mash to blend thoroughly. Spread the egg-butter mixture in a small serving bowl. Mix onion with sour cream and spoon over egg mixture. Refrigerate overnight. To serve, top with caviar and pass with melba toast.

3 hard-boiled eggs
¼ pound butter, softened
1 medium onion, finely chopped
1 cup sour cream
4-6 ounces black caviar
Melba toast

Arminda du Pont

CHEESE STRAWS

Yield: 9 dozen
Preparation: 20 minutes (plus refrigeration overnight)
Baking: 8-10 minutes

Grate cheese on grater in food processor. Using steel blade of food processor, mix all ingredients together (2 batches in small processor). Chill dough overnight. Divide dough into 3 or 4 portions. Soften just enough to roll out ⅛- to ¼-inch thick between two sheets of waxed paper. Using knife or tool with serrated edge, cut into strips 3 inches long and less than 1 inch wide. Place on ungreased cookie sheets. Bake at 400° until barely tan in color, about 8 to 10 minutes, watching carefully to be sure they do not burn.

1 pound extra sharp New York State cheese
1¾ cups flour
¾ cup butter
A few dashes cayenne

Harriot Kimmel

Chinese export porcelain geese, 1738-60

CHUTNEY-CURRY CHEESE SPREAD

Preparation: 10 minutes (plus 4-12 hours refrigeration)

Soften cream cheese in small mixing bowl. Add chutney, curry, and mustard and blend. Chill at least four hours or overnight. Cut pineapple in half leaving leaves on. Scoop out pineapple and put cheese spread in. Decorate with sliced almonds. If doubling, add an extra ½ teaspoon of curry powder and 2 tablespoons of chutney.

8 ounces cream cheese
¼ cup chutney, cut up
1 teaspoon curry powder
¼ teaspoon dry mustard
1 fresh pineapple
¼ cup sliced almonds, toasted (optional)

Mrs. Daniel M. Thornton III

CRAB AND CREAM CHEESE SPREAD

Preparation: 15 minutes
Baking: 15 minutes

Combine all ingredients. Put in ovenproof dish. Sprinkle with 1/3 cup toasted sliced almonds. Bake at 375° for 15 minutes.

8 ounces cream cheese
1 tablespoon milk
6½ ounces crab meat
2 tablespoons chopped onion
½ teaspoon cream-style horseradish
¼ teaspoon salt
Dash of pepper
1/3 cup sliced almonds, toasted

Huddie Shellenberger

BLUE GRASS DIP

Yield: 1½ cups
Preparation: 10 minutes (plus refrigeration)

Mix all ingredients together; refrigerate. Serve with raw vegetables or crackers.

1 package frozen chopped spinach, thawed and drained
4 tablespoons sour cream
2 tablespoons mayonnaise
4 ounces blue cheese, crumbled
½ can water chestnuts, sliced
Salt to taste

Betsy Cook

MUSHROOM CRACKER SPREAD

Preparation: 20 minutes
Cooking: 30 minutes

Cook bacon until crisp. Drain, crumble, and set aside. Cook mushrooms, onion, and garlic in bacon drippings until tender and liquid is evaporated. Stir in flour, salt, and pepper. Add cream cheese, Worcestershire sauce, and soy sauce. Heat and stir until cream cheese melts. Stir in sour cream and crumbled bacon. Heat but do not boil. Can be served warm or cold on crackers. Can be molded if served cold.

4 slices bacon
1 pound mushrooms, finely chopped (can be done in blender)
1 medium onion, chopped
1 clove garlic, minced
2 tablespoons flour
½ teaspoon salt
¼ teaspoon pepper
8 ounces cream cheese, cubed
2 teaspoons Worcestershire sauce
1 teaspoon soy sauce
½ cup sour cream

Elizabeth Tufts Brown

SALMON SPREAD

Yield: 2 balls
Preparation: 10 minutes (plus 4 hours refrigeration)
Freeze: Yes

Blend all ingredients except pecans and parsley. Chill for at least 4 hours. Divide in half, making two balls. Roll each ball in 3 tablespoons of chopped pecans mixed with 3 tablespoons of chopped parsley just before serving.

1 16-ounce can red salmon, drained, flaked, and bones removed
8 ounces cream cheese, softened
1 tablespoon lemon juice
¼ teaspoon salt
1 tablespoon white horseradish
2 tablespoons grated onion
½ tablespoon liquid smoke (optional)
6 tablespoons chopped pecans
6 tablespoons chopped parsley

Joy Hartshorn

The spring beauty of the Winterthur Gardens is preserved year-round in the Conservatory adjacent to Montmorenci Stairhall. The area, which abounds with greenery and flowers throughout the year, becomes a highlight of the museum tour at Christmas when it is filled with poinsettias and a tall Christmas tree. In the spring, the display of azaleas complements the azaleas outdoors.

The Conservatory is an ideal setting for an elegant dinner for two served on "Famille Rose," a Chinese export porcelain named for its predominant rosy color. This service dates from between 1740 and 1760 and is decorated with pink peonies — a favorite motif — and a decorative gilt border alternating with blue reserves. The table setting includes plates, soup plates filled with Quick Spinach Soup, a covered tureen, wooden-handled ladle, and candlesticks. Also displayed: silver forks with fiddle-shaped handles, made by Thomas Harland of Norwich, Connecticut, 1795-1807; pistol-handled knives made by Andrew E. Warner of Baltimore, Maryland, ca. 1828; enamel-twist wine glasses made in England, 1750-80. The wrought-iron chairs were made in the United States between 1875 and 1925 and have central scrolled hearts, serpentine crest rails, and iron "caned" seats.

ARTICHOKE-OYSTER SOUP

Serves: 8 (for first course)
Cooking: 35 minutes (8 hours before serving)

In a heavy 4-quart pot, melt butter and sauté chopped green onions and garlic until soft. Wash and drain artichokes. Cut each into 4 pieces and add to onions. Sprinkle with flour and stir to coat well. Do not brown. Add chicken stock, red pepper, anise seed, salt, and Worcestershire sauce. Simmer for about 15 minutes. While mixture cooks, drain oysters, reserve the liquor, and check oysters for shells. To chop oysters, put in blender. Without removing hand from switch, turn motor on and off twice. Add oysters and oyster liquor to pot. Simmer for about 10 minutes. Do not boil. This soup improves with age and should be made at least 8 hours before serving. Refrigerate, then reheat to serve. Keeps well 2 to 3 days. Excellent served as an appetizer.

¼ pound butter
2 bunches green onions, chopped
2 cloves garlic
3 14-ounce cans artichoke hearts
3 tablespoons flour
4 cans chicken stock
1 teaspoon red pepper flakes
1 teaspoon anise seed (or to taste)
1 teaspoon salt (or to taste)
1 tablespoon Worcestershire sauce
1 quart oysters

Janet M. Lemons

CREAM OF MUSHROOM SOUP

Serves: 6-8
Preparation: 30 minutes
Cooking: 15 minutes

Sauté onions, carrots, and celery in butter; add chopped mushrooms and a dash of Kitchen Bouquet. Blend in remaining ingredients.

½ cup butter
1/3 cup onions, chopped
¼ cup carrots, chopped
2/3 cup celery, chopped
1½ pounds mushrooms, chopped
Small amount of Kitchen Bouquet
¾ cup flour
3 cups chicken stock
2 cups milk
¼ teaspoon nutmeg
⅛ teaspoon paprika
3 tablespoons parsley, chopped
Dry sherry to taste

Mrs. Henry S. McNeil

PUMPKIN-MUSHROOM SOUP

Yield: 3 quarts
Preparation: 30 minutes
Cooking: 30 minutes
Freeze: Yes

In a large Dutch oven, sauté onions in butter until translucent. Stir in dry ingredients until mixture bubbles. Add chicken broth, water, and pumpkin; cook 10 to 15 minutes. At this point, the soup may be run through a blender and then a sieve to make the soup smooth, if desired. Again in the Dutch oven, add cream and milk to the pumpkin mixture. Bring to a boil. Add mushrooms. Allow to cook until mushrooms darken and become soft. To serve, ladle soup into bowls and top with a heaping teaspoon of sour cream and a sprinkling of fresh parsley. Croutons make a nice condiment. If freezing, mushrooms should be omitted until soup is thawed.

- **1-2 cups onion, finely chopped**
- **¼ cup butter**
- **Scant ¼ cup flour**
- **½ teaspoon salt**
- **½ teaspoon pepper**
- **½ teaspoon ginger**
- **½ teaspoon nutmeg**
- **2 10½-ounce cans double-strength chicken broth**
- **1 10½-ounce can water**
- **1 28-ounce can prepared pumpkin**
- **1 cup light cream and 1 cup milk or 2 cups half-and-half**
- **¼ pound fresh mushrooms, sliced**
- **Optional garnishes: sour cream, chopped fresh parsley, croutons**

"This soup is good as a first course for dinner or as a luncheon main course, served with salad and bread."
    Julia Hofer

FISHBERRY SOUP

Serves: 4
Preparation: 20-30 minutes
Cooking: 5-10 minutes
Freeze: Yes

Heat chicken stock. Add sugar, salt, pepper, garlic, and basil. Cook for 5 minutes. Strain the stock through a fine cloth or sieve. Add wine and heat thoroughly. After pouring the soup into bowls, carefully place a spoonful of caviar in the bottom of each bowl. The caviar will disperse slightly, giving a warm, red glow through the pale stock. The caviar will add saltiness to the soup, so be careful not to over salt. Seasoned stock freezes well, but do not add caviar until just before serving.

- **5 cups chicken stock**
- **4 teaspoons sugar**
- **½ teaspoon salt**
- **⅛ teaspoon black pepper, freshly ground (or to taste)**
- **2 cloves garlic, crushed**
- **4 fresh basil leaves (or dried basil to taste)**
- **½ cup dry vermouth**
- **1 small jar red caviar**

Rosemary Krill

LEARNED FISH CHOWDER

Serves: 4
Preparation: 40 minutes
Cooking: 2 hours
Freeze: Yes

Chop salt pork into very small squares. Melt down in frying pan until slightly colored. Remove pieces from pan and set aside. Slice potatoes and onions as thin as possible. Place potatoes in 2 quarts of heavily salted boiling water. Sauté onions in liquid from salt pork until translucent and add to potatoes. Cook 2 hours at a medium boil. Add fish and seasonings and cook until fish separates, approximately 8 to 10 minutes (frozen fish takes longer). Add cream and stir. Sprinkle pieces of salt pork into each bowl before adding chowder; dust paprika on top. Serve with salad and pilot or water biscuits. Stock can be frozen prior to adding fish and cream.

1 piece fatty salt pork (approximately 2 ounces)
9-10 medium potatoes
10-12 medium onions
1½-1¾ pounds fresh flounder (fluke or haddock may be substituted)
Salt
Pepper
½ pint light cream
Paprika

"Servings based on two large bowls per person using chowder as a main course; New England Sunday night supper."
Mrs. John Learned

SHERRIED MUSHROOM CONSOMME

Serves: 6
Cooking: 20 minutes

Sauté onion in butter until clear but not brown. Add mushrooms and cook 5 minutes. Add stock and sherry. Garnish with watercress.

1 small onion, minced
2 tablespoons butter
¾ pound mushrooms, thinly sliced
1 quart brown stock, clarified
2 tablespoons sherry
Chopped watercress

Lorraine Siltzer

Chinese export porcelain goose tureen, 1750-70

INDIAN CRAB SOUP

Serves: 6
Preparation: 10 minutes
Cooking: 25 minutes

Melt butter and add onion, cooking until transparent. Stir in garlic and apple. Sprinkle with curry and flour. Add tomato and chicken broth. Whisk. When thickened and smooth, add salt and pepper, crab, and simmer 10 minutes. Add cream and bring to a boil. Add Tabasco sauce. Garnish with sour cream.

4 tablespoons butter
½ cup onion, finely chopped
1 clove garlic, minced
1 medium apple, peeled and diced
2 teaspoons curry powder
3 tablespoons flour
1 medium tomato, peeled and chopped
3 cups chicken broth
Salt and pepper to taste
½ pound crab meat
½ cup heavy cream
Dash of Tabasco sauce
Sour cream

Wylma P. Davis

LENTIL SOUP

Serves: 6-8
Preparation: 20 minutes
Cooking: 2 hours

Sauté bacon, carrots, onion, celery, and garlic until golden. Combine with lentils, water, stock, tomato paste, bouquet garni, salt, and pepper. Cover and bring to a boil, simmering 1½ hours. Add potatoes, bring to a boil and cook 20 minutes. Remove bouquet garni. Season with vinegar and adjust with salt and pepper. Sprinkle with lots of slivered green onions and grated Cheddar cheese. Top with sour cream.

4 slices bacon, minced
½ cup each diced carrots and onions
¾ cup diced celery
1 garlic clove, minced
1 cup lentils
2 cups water
3 cups beef stock
¼ cup tomato paste
Bouquet garni of 3 cloves, 1 bay leaf, 3 parsley sprigs, 1 thyme sprig
½ teaspoon salt
¼ teaspoon pepper
1 ½ cups diced potato
1 ½ tablespoons red wine vinegar
Slivered green onions
Cheddar cheese
Sour cream

CREAM OF WILD RICE SOUP

Serves: 4 as entree; 8 as soup course
Preparation: 20 minutes (plus refrigeration)
Cooking: 40-50 minutes

Rinse rice in sieve under cold running water. Put rice, water, and ½ teaspoon salt into 2-quart saucepan and bring to boil. Reduce heat, cover, and simmer 30 to 40 minutes until rice is tender and kernels begin to pop. Melt butter in heavy 4-quart pot or Dutch oven. Add onion and celery. Cover and cook gently about 5 minutes until vegetables are soft. Stir in 1 teaspoon salt, pepper and flour. Remove from heat and add milk, 1 tablespoon at a time at first, stirring until flour is well blended. Return pot to low heat and cook, stirring constantly until soup thickens. Add rice and simmer for a few minutes to heat through. Serve in bowls or cups with garnish of scallions. This soup is best when made 6 to 24 hours ahead and refrigerated for flavors to blend. Reheat slowly at low temperature, stirring often. If soup has thickened too much, it can be diluted with a little milk.

1/3 cup wild rice
1 cup water
1½ teaspoon salt
½ cup butter
1 cup finely chopped onion
1 cup finely sliced celery
½ teaspoon pepper
¼ cup flour
5 cups milk
Optional garnish: finely sliced scallions

"This soup makes an elegant 'Tureen Supper,' served with cold shrimp or crab appetizer as a first course, a fresh spinach salad, and hot corn muffins."
Joyce Ford Halbrook

SQUASH SOUP

Serves: 4-6
Preparation: 30 minutes (plus refrigeration, if desired)
Cooking: 5 minutes

Purée squash in blender. Add bouillon and half-and-half. Blend. Add parsley for a very short time. Do not fully blend. It gives a peppery taste without adding pepper. Serve hot or cold.

1-1½ cups yellow summer squash, cooked with onion (leftover or freshly cooked)
2 cups chicken bouillon
1 cup half-and-half
1 handful parsley tips

"Surprising taste, lovely color, and as good cold as hot."
Margaret Symonds

CUBAN BLACK BEAN SOUP

Serves: 4-6
Cooking: 3 ½ hours

Soak beans overnight in cold water up to rim of container. Drain. Place beans in kettle with 1 ½ quarts of water. Add ham bone; cover and simmer until beans are soft (approximately 3 hours). Remove ham bone. Heat olive oil in a skillet and sauté onion and green pepper until tender. Stir in crushed garlic and cumin seeds. Add mixture to beans, along with tomato, salt, and pepper. Simmer the soup over very low heat for 30 minutes. Add wine or rum to taste. Serve in bowls with a large spoonful of rice in each bowl. Pass the condiments.

½ pound dried black beans
1 ham bone
4 tablespoons olive oil
1 large onion, chopped
1 green pepper, chopped
Salt and pepper
2 cloves garlic, crushed
1 teaspoon cumin seed
**1 large tomato, peeled and
    chopped**
Salt and pepper to taste
Madeira, sherry, or rum
1½ cups rice, cooked
**Condiments: chopped onion,
    sliced lemon, chopped egg,
    parsley, sliced avocado,
    cooked and crumbled
    bacon, and shredded
    Cheddar or Monterey Jack
    cheese**

Anne Beckley Coleman

QUICK SPINACH SOUP

Serves: 4
Cooking: 10 minutes

Cook spinach in stock until almost done. Drop egg into boiling pot. Stir. Add salt. Top with Parmesan cheese and serve.

1 package frozen spinach
1 quart chicken stock
1 egg, slightly beaten
Salt to taste
**Parmesan cheese, freshly
    grated**

Beverly Butler Lane

Pewter porringer made by Frederick Bassett, 1761-1800

HUGER VEGETABLE SOUP

Yield: 2 gallons
Cooking: All day
Freeze: Yes

Remove gristle from beef. Boil beef and bones in water at least 2 hours. Do not season. Add okra. Boil 15 to 30 minutes. Add tomatoes, reserving juice from 1 can. Reduce to medium heat and cook until okra and tomatoes begin to fall apart, approximately 30 minutes. Add salt and Worcestershire sauce. Remove bones and add corn. (Note: Start stirring more frequently since corn sticks to bottom easily. If corn sticks, do not scrape. Leave and pour off soup when finished.) Simmer about 1 hour until soup is very thick when stirred. Add ketchup. Correct seasonings to taste. Use additional tomato juice if liquid is needed. Soup should be consistency of a thick Brunswick stew. Serve over rice with diced green pepper. If started in afternoon, cover, and place in oven overnight, continuing in morning.

3 pounds lean stew beef cut into 2 inch chunks
1-2 soup bones
1 gallon water
4 boxes frozen cut okra
2 20-ounce cans whole tomatoes, peeled
1 teaspoon salt
4 tablespoons Worcestershire sauce
4 1-pound cans white cream-style corn
12 ounces ketchup
1 package frozen baby limas (optional)
1 package frozen whole green beans (optional)
Rice
Green pepper, diced

Mrs. J. Ray Efird

CUCUMBER SOUP

Serves: 4-6
Preparation: 15 minutes (plus refrigeration)
Cooking: 5 minutes
Freeze: Yes

Place all ingredients except salt and pepper in blender and blend until smooth. Pour into saucepan and heat to boiling, stirring constantly. Add salt and pepper. Chill and serve with thin slices of lemon and bits of parsley. To freeze, blend all ingredients except cream. Add cream after thawing. Heat to boiling, then serve hot or chilled.

2 cups cucumber, coarsely chopped (seeds removed and partially pared)
1 cup chicken stock
2 tablespoons chives, chopped
¼ cup celery leaves, chopped
¼ cup parsley, chopped
2 tablespoons butter, softened
2 tablespoons flour
1 cup light cream
½ teaspoon salt
¼ teaspoon pepper
1 lemon, thinly sliced
Parsley

Mrs. Henry T. Skinner

ONION SOUP AU GRATIN

Serves: 4
Cooking: 45-55 minutes

Melt butter and heat the oil in a casserole. Add the onions, salt, and pepper. Sauté slowly until onions are dark brown, approximately 20 to 30 minutes. Add flour and mustard and stir until smooth. Continue stirring while adding the wine and stock, and bring slowly to a boil. Simmer 15 minutes. Put thick slices of toasted French bread into soup bowl. Add soup. Sprinkle the top with grated Swiss cheese and brown quickly under the broiler. Sprinkle sliced French bread with oil and the Parmesan. Brown in the oven and serve separately.

4 tablespoons butter
2 tablespoons vegetable oil
6 medium onions, finely sliced
Salt and pepper
1 teaspoon flour
½ teaspoon Dijon-style mustard
½ cup dry white wine
2½ cups stock or water
4 tablespoons grated Swiss cheese
4 tablespoons grated Parmesan cheese
French bread

Mrs. Blanche Gibbs

SHRIMP BISQUE

Serves: 6
Preparation: 20 minutes
Cooking: 30 minutes

Sauté shrimp and vegetables in butter over low heat about 2 minutes. Stir in salt, cayenne, and chicken broth. Bring to a boil and cook 20 minutes. Pour shrimp mixture into electric blender; blend until smooth. Combine shrimp purée, light cream, and wine in a saucepan; heat thoroughly. Serve immediately.

2 pounds raw shrimp, peeled and chopped
¼ cup chopped mushrooms
2 tablespoons chopped onion
2 tablespoons chopped celery
1 tablespoon chopped carrot
3 tablespoons melted butter
Salt to taste
Cayenne pepper to taste
2 cups chicken broth
1½ cups light cream
½ cup dry white wine

Beverley Brainard Fleming

Silver ladle with wooden handle, 1720-50

ONION SOUP WITH PUFFY CHEESE CROUTONS

Serves: 6-8
Preparation: 10 minutes
Cooking: 40-45 minutes

SOUP:

Sauté onion in butter until limp but not brown; blend in flour. Add broth and water; stir until smooth. Simmer about 30 minutes. Serve soup with Puffy Cheese Croutons.

SOUP:
4 cups thinly sliced onions
¼ cup melted butter
2 tablespoons flour
2 10½-ounce cans condensed beef broth, undiluted
1 10¾-ounce can condensed chicken broth, undiluted
1 soup can water

PUFFY CHEESE CROUTONS:

Melt butter in top of double boiler over hot, but not boiling, water or in a saucepan over very low heat. Add milk and cheese, stirring constantly until cheese is melted. Remove from heat. Beat egg whites until stiff, but not dry; gently fold into cheese mixture. Cut 30 bite-sized cubes of french bread; dip into egg-cheese mixture. Bake on ungreased cookie sheet at 400° for 10 to 15 minutes or until lightly browned. Remove from oven immediately.

PUFFY CHEESE CROUTONS:
¼ cup butter
1 tablespoon milk
1 cup shredded Cheddar cheese
2 egg whites
French bread

Beverley Brainard Fleming

CORN CHOWDER

Serves: 6
Preparation: 20 minutes
Cooking: 30 minutes
Freeze: Yes

Sauté bacon and onion and set aside. Boil potatoes in water until tender, about 15 minutes. Add remaining ingredients except cheese. Simmer until heated through. Do not boil. Put cubed cheese in bowls. Ladle hot soup over cheese and serve.

4 slices bacon, chopped
1 medium onion, chopped
2 cups diced potatoes
2 cups water
Salt and pepper to taste
2 cups cream-style corn
1½ cups milk
½ cup evaporated milk or half-and-half
1 tablespoon butter
Sharp Cheddar cheese, cubed

"Even better the second day."
   Mrs. Edgar Tufts

SHE-CRAB SOUP

Serves: 8-10
Cooking: 10-15 minutes

Combine first nine ingredients in a large Dutch oven; bring to a boil. Add crab meat; cook over medium heat, stirring occasionally, until thoroughly heated. Stir in sherry. Sprinkle each serving with marigold leaves, if desired.

2 10¾-ounce cans cream of
  celery soup, undiluted
3 cups milk
1 cup half-and-half
½ cup butter
2 hard-boiled eggs, chopped
½ teaspoon Old Bay seasoning
½ teaspoon Worcestershire
  sauce
¼ teaspoon garlic salt
¼ teaspoon white pepper
1 cup crab meat, drained and
  flaked
¼ cup dry sherry
Marigold leaves (optional)

Beverley Brainard Fleming

SPECIAL CHICKEN SOUP

Serves: 6-8
Cooking: 30-40 minutes

Cook onion and ham in butter until onion is wilted. Add chicken stock and bouquet garni. Simmer for 20 minutes and remove herbs. Mix together egg yolks, cream, and cheeses. Mix a cup of the hot stock into this, then stir in the remaining soup. Heat, correct seasoning, strain, and garnish with paprika.

1 cup chopped onion
2 tablespoons minced ham
3 tablespoons butter
2 ounces freshly grated
  Parmesan cheese
1 bouquet garni (parsley,
  rosemary, small piece bay
  leaf, 1 blade mace)
3 egg yolks
1 cup heavy cream
4 cups chicken stock
1 ounce grated Gruyère
Paprika

Mrs. Patricia Seballoz

VICHYSSOISE

Serves: 12
Cooking: 1 hour (plus overnight refrigeration)

Melt butter in 3-quart saucepan. Add leeks and onions and simmer for 10 minutes or until half cooked. Add chicken broth and potatoes, salt and pepper, and simmer for 30 to 40 minutes. Add milk and bring to a boil. Taste for seasoning, then purée in blender. Chill overnight. When the soup is cold and ready to serve, add cream. Add chives if desired. Serve in cold cups.

2 tablespoons sweet butter
6 leeks, white part only, finely sliced
2 small onions, finely sliced
2 quarts chicken broth
5 medium-sized potatoes, finely sliced
Salt and pepper
2 cups milk, scalded
1 cup light cream
Chives, finely chopped (optional)

Winterthur Archives ℳ

TANGY ICED TOMATO SOUP

Serves: 4
Cooking: 8 minutes (plus refrigeration)

Combine tomatoes, onions, water, salt and pepper in a saucepan. Cook over moderate heat 5 minutes. Combine tomato paste and flour; add to chicken stock. Stir into hot mixture. Simmer gently 3 minutes. Process in blender or press through sieve until pureed. Chill thoroughly. Just before serving add cream and lemon juice. Garnish with a thin slice of tomato or sprig of parsley if desired.

4 large ripe tomatoes, peeled, seeded and chopped
1 small onion, chopped
½ cup water
¼ teaspoon salt
⅛ teaspoon pepper
2 tablespoons tomato paste
2 teaspoons flour
2 cups strained chicken stock (fat removed)
2/3 cup heavy cream
Juice of ½ lemon
Parsley (optional)

Kate Wheeler

Iron broiler, 1760-1820

ICED LEMON SOUP

Serves: 4-6
Preparation: 15 minutes (plus refrigeration)

Place all ingredients in a blender. Blend until smooth. Refrigerate in quart jars until very cold. Serve in ice cold cups.

1 can cream of chicken soup
1 cup cream
1 cup chicken stock
3 tablespoons chopped mint
Juice of 1-2 lemons
Garnish: chopped mint, chives, paprika, or a thin lemon slice

"A refreshing and appetizing start to a hot weather meal."
  Betty Garrigues

GAZPACHO

Serves: 4-6
Preparation: 10 minutes (plus 6 hours refrigeration)

Mix all ingredients except croutons in a bowl and chill 6 hours. Just before serving, garnish with croutons.

1 14-ounce can tomatoes, undrained
1 medium green pepper, chopped
½ cucumber, peeled and sliced
½ cup onion, chopped
2 tablespoons oil
2 tablespoon wine vinegar
1 teaspoon salt
1 teaspoon sugar
Tabasco sauce (optional)
½ cup croutons

"This is a great summer treat. Tastes just like a liquid tossed salad."
  Beverly Vermilyea

Porcelain ox tureen, 1750-70

Salads & Dressings

The most beautiful cut glass of the eighteenth and nineteenth centuries was made in England and Ireland. The brilliance and sparkle of glass was enhanced by cutting angular incisions that act as prisms. The cutting was done by revolving wheels that ground away the surface of the glass where it had been marked by the craftsman. After this the rough pattern was smoothed and polished.

California Salad is served in a boat-shaped salad or fruit bowl cut in a pattern of diamonds and flutes, made in Ireland, ca. 1800. The bowl has the solid diamond-shaped stand and scalloped rim often found on this type of vessel. The table is also set with cut-glass, ogee-profile plates, made either in England or Ireland between 1780 and 1800. Also shown are silver and glass condiment bottles made in London, 1774-75, in a silver cruet stand made by John David of Philadelphia, ca. 1763; the silver forks were made by Hugh Wisnart of New York, 1810-19. The linen napkin with floral damask design was made in the United States, 1830-40, and the silver serving spoon was made by Shepherd and Boyd of Albany, New York, ca. 1820.

BEACH SLAW

Serves: 12
Preparation: 20 minutes (with food processor)
Cooking: 10 minutes

Put first four ingredients in a large bowl. Bring remaining ingredients to a boil. Pour over chopped vegetables and let stand until cool. Cover and refrigerate. This crispy salad keeps well in the refrigerator two weeks or more.

1 medium-sized cabbage, grated
1 green pepper, chopped
1 cup grated onion
1 3-ounce jar pimentos, chopped
2 cups sugar
2 cups vinegar
1 teaspoon salt
1 teaspoon tumeric
1 teaspoon mustard seed
1 teaspoon celery seed

Sis Bancroft

TACO SALAD

Serves: 8-10
Preparation: 40 minutes
Cooking: 5 minutes

Brown ground beef in skillet and drain off excess fat. Cook briefly with chili powder and garlic. Set aside to cool. Combine lettuce, olives, cheese, scallions, beans, tomatoes, avocado, and salt. Add beef mixture and stir.

1 pound lean ground beef
4 teaspoons chili powder
1 clove garlic, minced
Half a head lettuce, chopped
1 cup black olives, pitted and sliced
8 ounces sharp Cheddar cheese, grated
5 scallions, chopped
1 can red kidney beans, drained
2 ripe tomatoes, chopped
1 avocado, peeled and diced
1 teaspoon salt
2 cups corn chips, crumbled

DRESSING:
Mix all ingredients. Add crushed corn chips and dressing to salad immediately before serving and mix well.

DRESSING:
½ cup tomato juice
1 tablespoon Tabasco sauce (or 2 small green chili peppers, chopped)
1 tablespoon olive oil
Juice of ½ lemon
Salt and pepper to taste

Ellen and Bert Denker

MARINATED VEGETABLE SALAD

Serves: 8
Preparation: 20 minutes (one day in advance of serving)

Mix vegetables. Marinate in a well-flavored oil and vinegar dressing (garlic flavor is recommended). Serve without lettuce in a large glass bowl.

2 10-ounce packages frozen peas, thawed
1 7-ounce can water chestnuts, diced
1 7-ounce can black olives, pitted
1 bunch scallions, sliced
1 4-ounce can pimentos, sliced
1 ½ cups raw mushrooms, sliced
Oil and vinegar dressing

Joyce McClung

SEAFOOD MELANGE

Serves: 6
Preparation: 1 hour (one day in advance of serving)

Cook and drain macaroni shells following directions on package. Cook shrimp. Add remaining ingredients and toss. Sprinkle with paprika and refrigerate. Salad is best if prepared and put in the refrigerator overnight.

1 pound shell macaroni
1 cup shrimp, cooked and peeled
2 stalks of celery, chopped
1 small onion, chopped
½ green pepper, chopped
2 tablespoons pimento, diced
1 small can tuna, flaked
⅛ teaspoon white pepper
⅛ teaspoon flavor enhancer
⅛ teaspoon celery salt
¼ teaspoon seasoned salt
⅛ teaspoon oregano
⅛ teaspoon dry mustard
⅛ teaspoon paprika
1 heaping tablespoon prepared mustard
2 heaping tablespoons sweet relish
2 hard-boiled eggs, diced
1 small can crabmeat
4 tablespoons mayonnaise
Additional paprika

Carol Goble

SPINACH
AND SPROUT SALAD

Serves: 8
Preparation: 30 minutes to 1 hour
Cooking: 5 minutes

Toss spinach, water chestnuts, bean sprouts, mushrooms, eggs, and bacon in a salad bowl.

1 pound spinach, washed and torn into pieces
1 5-ounce can water chestnuts, drained and sliced
1 cup bean sprouts
½ pound fresh mushrooms, sliced
4 hard-boiled eggs, chopped
8 slices bacon, cooked and crumbled

DRESSING:
Combine ingredients and heat to simmer. Pour as much dressing on salad as desired. Mix and serve at once.

DRESSING:
½ cup salad oil
¼ cup bacon drippings
1/3 cup ketchup
¼ cup vinegar
¼ cup sugar
½ medium onion, grated
1 tablespoon Worcestershire sauce

"Nutritious and so good!"
    Anne Y. Wolfe

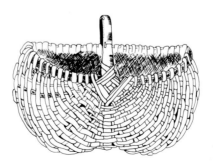

Wood splint basket, 1800-1900

MARINATED ARTICHOKE HEARTS

Serves: 8
Preparation: 15 minutes (one day in advance of serving)

Slice artichoke hearts into halves and drain. Mix oil, lemon juice, sugar, salt, mustard, pepper, basil, and garlic. Stir in artichoke hearts, mushrooms, and pimento. Toss mixture and cover. Prepare early in the day or a day ahead.

2 14-ounce cans artichoke hearts
¾ cup salad oil
½ cup lemon juice
1 tablespoon sugar
2 teaspoons salt
1 teaspoon dry mustard
½ teaspoon pepper
½ teaspoon basil
1 small clove garlic, crushed
1 pound mushrooms, sliced
2 tablespoons diced pimento

Mrs. Steven Pulinka

CONFETTI RICE SALAD

Serves: 8
Preparation: 30 minutes

Place cooked rice and peas in large bowl and let cool. Add scallions, dressing, mayonnaise, and pimentos. Toss together, add spices to taste, and chill.

2 cups cooked rice
2 10-ounce packages frozen peas, cooked as directed
1 bunch scallions, minced with green stems
1 cup Italian salad dressing
1 cup mayonnaise
4 ounces pimento, diced
Salt, pepper and garlic salt to taste

Debbie Kassner

Cut glass bowl, ca. 1800

POTATO SALAD

Serves: 4-6
Preparation: 2-3 hours

Mix well vinegar, oil, salt, sugar, and mustard. Pour over potatoes and carrots. Chill 2 to 3 hours then add onion and eggs. Combine mayonnaise and cream and add to mixture just before serving.

3 tablespoons vinegar
2 tablespoons salad oil
2 teaspoons salt
½ teaspoon sugar (or more to taste)
2 teaspoons mustard
6 potatoes, diced and cooked
1½ cups carrots, sliced and cooked (optional)
1 tablespoon minced onion
4 hard-boiled eggs, diced
2/3 cup mayonnaise
¼ cup light cream

Erma Schlegel Bowen

MUSHROOM SALAD FINLANDIA

Serves: 4
Preparation: 10 minutes

Boil water with lemon juice. Add mushrooms, cover, and simmer 2 to 3 minutes. Drain. Combine other ingredients except lettuce. Toss mushrooms carefully in dressing and serve on crisp lettuce leaves.

1 cup water
1 tablespoon lemon juice
½ pound fresh mushrooms, thinly sliced
1/3 cup sour cream
2 tablespoons grated onion
½ teaspoon salt
Freshly ground black pepper to taste
Romaine lettuce

Dena N. Forster

Tin-glazed earthenware tankard with pewter lid, c. 1743

CALIFORNIA SALAD

Serves: 4-5
Preparation: 30 minutes

Cook shrimp in boiling water for 2 minutes; plunge into cold water. Shell shrimp, leaving tails on. Cut grapefruits in half and remove sections to large bowl. Peel oranges and divide into sections, leaving membranes on; add to grapefruit. Add onion and shrimp to fruit. Prior to serving, slice avocado and toss with other ingredients. Serve on lettuce and dress with Celery Seed Dressing.

1 pound shrimp
2-3 grapefruits
4-5 navel oranges
1 large Spanish onion, sliced
2 avocados
Leaf lettuce
Celery Seed Dressing

Kay T. Beckley

AVOCADO PEARS FLORIDA

Serves: 12
Preparation: 30 minutes

Avocados must be ripe, perfect, and cold. Cut in halves and remove the seeds. With a teaspoon, scallop the inside without removing it. Make a dressing of mayonnaise, chili sauce, Worcestershire sauce, and lemon juice. Pass through a strainer and keep on ice. Clean crab meat of all foreign substances. Mix gently with 2/3 of the dressing and fill each avocado half. With a tablespoon, spread the remaining dressing on each avocado. Garnish each with an anchovy fillet cut into slices. Serve very cold.

6 small avocados
2 cups mayonnaise
3 tablespoons chili sauce
Dash of Worcestershire sauce
Dash of lemon juice
1 pound crab meat
12 fillets of anchovies

Winterthur Archives

FRESH BROCCOLI SALAD

Serves: 8
Preparation: 10 minutes (two hours in advance)

Wash and cut broccoli into bite-sized pieces. Combine broccoli, bacon, raisins, and onion. In another bowl, combine mayonnaise, sugar, and vinegar; mix well. Pour dressing over broccoli mixture and toss. Refrigerate two hours before serving, tossing occasionally.

2 bunches fresh broccoli
10 slices bacon, cooked and crumbled
2/3 cup raisins
½ onion, chopped
1 cup mayonnaise
½ cup sugar
2 tablespoons vinegar

Mrs. Steven Pulinka

MAX'S SPINACH SALAD
WITH GARLIC VINAIGRETTE

Serves: 4-6
Preparation: 30 minutes

SPINACH SALAD:
Tear spinach into bite-sized pieces. Place in serving bowl. Sprinkle eggs and bacon over top. Pour dressing over salad, toss lightly, and serve at once.

GARLIC VINAIGRETTE:
Using either a small bowl and wire whisk or a covered jar, thoroughly blend vinegar, salt, and mustard. Add oil and mix completely. Add pepper to taste. Refrigerate. Add garlic to dressing about 2 hours before serving. Just before serving, strain and pour desired amount of dressing over salad. Makes about 1 cup.

Robert L. Maxwell

SPINACH SALAD:
1 pound fresh spinach, washed well and drained
3 hard-boiled eggs, chopped
8 slices bacon, cooked and crumbled

GARLIC VINAIGRETTE:
3 tablespoons white wine vinegar
½ teaspoon salt
1½ teaspoons Dijon-style mustard
¾ cup oil
Freshly ground black pepper to taste
3 cloves garlic, coarsely chopped

WALNUT AND
ROQUEFORT SALAD

Serves: 4-6
Cooking: 8 minutes

Toast walnut halves in heavy skillet until golden, 5 to 8 minutes. Cool. Mix vinegar, salt and pepper in a small bowl. Add oil in thin stream, whisking continuously until dressing is smooth and thoroughly blended. Combine romaine, chicory, avocado, scallions, cheese, and walnuts in salad bowl. Toss with dressing and serve.

½ cup walnut halves
5 tablespoons white wine vinegar
½ teaspoon salt
½ teaspoon pepper
½ cup olive oil
1 medium head romaine
½ head chicory
1 avocado, peeled, pitted, sliced, and dipped in lemon juice
2 scallions with tops, trimmed and chopped
4 ounces Roquefort cheese, crumbled

PERUVIAN POTATO SALAD

Serves: 6-8
Preparation: 35 minutes
(early in day)

Early in the day, cook potatoes, drain, peel, and slice ¼-inch thick. Potatoes may be marinated in oil and vinegar, if desired. Cool and refrigerate. One half hour before serving, shell eggs, halve, and remove yolks. Chop whites and set aside. Mash yolks, add next 6 ingredients, and beat until smooth. Gradually add oil while beating constantly. Blend in onion, celery and parsley. Arrange potatoes on lettuce-lined platter. Pour on dressing. Garnish with egg whites, olives, and parsley.

2 pounds medium-sized new potatoes
Oil and vinegar
3 hard-boiled eggs
16 ounces creamed cottage cheese
¼ teaspoon red pepper
Dash Tabasco sauce
⅛ teaspoon black pepper, freshly ground
1½ teaspoons salt
2 tablespoons heavy cream
1/3 cup oil
1 medium onion, finely chopped
¼ cup chopped celery
¼ cup chopped parsley
Black olives and parsley
Lettuce leaves

Dena N. Forster

SPINACH-SESAME SALAD

Serves: 4-6
Preparation: 30 minutes

Mix oil, soy sauce, vinegar, garlic, and seasonings. Pour over spinach. Sprinkle with sesame seed and egg. Toss lightly and serve at once.

¼ cup oil
2 tablespoons soy sauce
2 tablespoons wine vinegar
1 small clove garlic, crushed
¼ teaspoon salt
¼ teaspoon pepper
¼ teaspoon sugar
⅛ teaspoon ginger
½ pound spinach, washed and torn into pieces (6 cups packed)
2 tablespoons sesame seed, toasted
1 hard-boiled egg, chopped

Lela E. Lippert

AVOCADO
WITH HOT SAUCE

Serves: 6
Preparation: 15 minutes

Cut avocados in half; remove seeds and leave skin on. Place on watercress. For sauce, mix all remaining ingredients together in a double boiler. Serve very hot in pitcher or sauce boat.

3 avocados
Watercress
4 tablespoons butter
2 tablespoons water
4 tablespoons ketchup
2 tablespoons vinegar
3 teaspoons sugar
**2 teaspoons Worcestershire
   sauce**
1/3 teaspoon salt
Dash Tabasco sauce

Winterthur Archives

ARTICHOKE SALAD
WITH SNOW PEAS

Serves: 6-8
Preparation: 15 minutes

Combine first 3 ingredients in a large glass bowl. In a small bowl combine the next 7 ingredients and whisk in the half-and-half in a slow steady stream until well combined. Toss the vegetables with the dressing and toasted almonds.

**1 14-ounce can artichoke
   hearts, drained and halved**
**2 cups fresh mushrooms,
   thinly sliced**
**1½ cups snow peas, strings
   removed, trimmed, and cut
   into bite-sized pieces**
¼ cup red wine vinegar
¼ cup vegetable oil
**2 teaspoons Dijon-style
   mustard**
1 teaspoon garlic, minced
1 teaspoon dill weed
1 teaspoon salt
**Freshly ground black pepper
   to taste**
1 cup half-and-half
**2/3 cup sliced almonds,
   toasted**

Dena N. Forster

Red earthenware plate with yellow slip decoration, 1824

MARINATED MUSHROOMS

Yield: 16-20
Preparation: 30 minutes
(2 days in advance)

Wash and stem mushrooms. Combine other ingredients thoroughly and pour over mushroom caps. Refrigerate and marinate for two days.

3 pounds small mushrooms
1 cup grape seed oil
½ cup red wine vinegar
Salt and pepper to taste
1 tablespoon sugar
1 teaspoon Worcestershire sauce
2 medium onions, thinly sliced

Arminda du Pont

ITALIAN RICE SALAD

Serves: 8-10
Preparation: 30 minutes
Cooking 5 minutes

SALAD:
Sauté scallops in hot butter for about 3 minutes, just enough to cook them lightly. Combine scallops with remaining salad ingredients in serving bowl.

SALAD:
1 pound bay or calico scallops
5 cups cooked rice
1 pound shrimp, cooked, peeled and sliced in half lengthwise
2 tablespoons butter
1½ cups finely diced green pepper
¾ cup finely chopped red onion
1-1½ cups cooked and quartered artichoke hearts
¼ cup capers
1/3 cup chopped fresh parsley
1/3 cup chopped fresh dill

DRESSING:
Whisk oil with vinegar and beat in remaining dressing ingredients. Pour over salad and toss gently. Chill or serve at room temperature to enhance flavor.

DRESSING:
10 tablespoons olive oil
6-7 tablespoons red wine vinegar
Salt and freshly ground pepper to taste
2 large cloves garlic, minced
2 tablespoons chopped fresh basil
½ teaspoon dried oregano
2 tablespoons minced parsley

Sandra Hitchens

MOSTLY MUSHROOM SALAD

Serves: 6
Preparation: 20-25 minutes

Rinse, pat dry, and slice mushrooms. Place mushrooms, celery, green pepper, and onion in a salad bowl. Combine remaining ingredients and pour over vegetables. Toss gently and serve on lettuce.

1 pound fresh mushrooms, sliced (about 5 cups)
1 cup celery, diced
1 cup green pepper, diced
2 tablespoons red onion, finely chopped
2 tablespoons salad oil
1 tablespoon wine vinegar
1 teaspoon salt
⅛ teaspoon black pepper
2 tablespoons fresh lemon juice
Green leaf lettuce

"Delicious, light, low-calorie salad to accompany a meat or chicken dinner. Only 59 calories per portion."
   Ruth A. Hansen

SHRIMP RICE SALAD

Serves: 6
Preparation: 15 minutes

With stem ends down, cut tomatoes into six wedges, cutting to—but not through—bases. Scoop out pulp, dice, and drain. Chill tomato shells. Combine diced pulp, shrimp, rice, celery, olives, and parsley. Blend remaining ingredients. Toss gently with the shrimp mixture, adding salt and pepper to taste. Chill. Mound shrimp in tomato shells. Trim with watercress and additional shrimp.

6 large tomatoes
2 cups shrimp, cooked and peeled
1½ cups cooked rice
1/3 cup chopped celery
¾ cup black olives, pitted
1 tablespoon parsley, snipped
¼ cup salad oil
2 tablespoons red wine vinegar
1 small clove garlic, minced
¼ teaspoon dry mustard
¼ teaspoon paprika
½ teaspoon salt
Pepper
Watercress and additional shrimp

Jackie Kelly

MELON AND SHRIMP SALAD

Serves: 8-10
Preparation: 30 minutes
(plus refrigeration)

Use small European shrimp if available. Otherwise, chop larger shrimp into bite-sized pieces. Mix with the melon balls and celery. Combine sour cream, mayonnaise, dressing, and curry. Mixture should be consistency of light cream. Toss with shrimp mixture and refrigerate for several hours.

4½ pounds shrimp, cooked, peeled, and deveined
1 large melon, scooped into balls
¾ cup chopped celery
1 cup sour cream
½ cup mayonnaise
½ cup vinaigrette dressing
2 tablespoons curry powder (or to taste)

"Easy and refreshing."
   Annie Jones

COLD SALMON AND MACARONI SALAD

Serves: 6
Preparation time: 30 minutes
(plus 2 hours refrigeration)

Cook macaroni as directed on package. Drain and rinse macaroni thoroughly with cold water. Drain salmon and separate into chunks removing any bones. Combine cooked macaroni, salmon, eggs, onion and celery. Add 1 cup mayonnaise or more according to taste. Add red wine vinegar, if desired. Salt and pepper to taste. Chill at least 2 hours. Serve on a bed of lettuce with sliced garden tomatoes and crusty French bread.

1 15-½ ounce can red salmon
1 ½ cups uncooked elbow macaroni
1 medium onion, chopped
2-3 stalks celery, chopped
4-6 hard-boiled eggs, chopped
1 cup mayonnaise
1-2 tablespoons red wine vinegar (optional)
Salt and pepper
Lettuce
Tomatoes

"Great for dinner on a hot day."
   Maruta Skelton

Butter print, 1750-1850

CHICK PEA SALAD

Serves: 8-10
Preparation: 15 minutes (plus one hour refrigeration)

Combine first 5 ingredients in blender or shaker and mix until smooth. Combine chick peas and onion in a large bowl. Pour dressing over vegetables and toss. Refrigerate at least 1 hour (may be prepared to this point several days in advance). Just before serving add cheese and parsley; toss.

Dena N. Forster

2 teaspoons Dijon-style mustard
1½ teaspoons salt
½ cup olive oil
½ cup lemon juice
¼ teaspoon black pepper, freshly ground
2 20-ounce cans chick peas, drained
1 medium-sized red onion, chopped
½ pound feta cheese, crumbled
2 tablespoons chopped fresh parsley

ORIENTAL SWEET AND SOUR SALAD

Serves: 6
Preparation: 20 minutes (plus refrigeration)

Whisk all dressing ingredients (mayonnaise through curry powder) and chill. Prepare vegetables and almonds, toss with dressing, and serve.

Beverly Vermilyea

1¼ cups mayonnaise
½ cup vegetable oil
¼ cup honey
¼ cup Dijon-style mustard
3 tablespoons lemon juice
2 green onions, finely chopped
1 tablespoon fresh parsley, chopped
1 teaspoon celery seed
¼ teaspoon dry mustard
¼ teaspoon curry powder
2 packages fresh spinach, washed
4 ounces alfalfa sprouts
20 cherry tomatoes
1 cup slivered almonds

HEALTH FARM
FRUIT SALAD

Serves: 8-10
Preparation: 20 minutes

SALAD:
Place salad ingredients in large bowl. Mix dressing.
Pour over salad, toss well, and serve.

SALAD:
1 pint blueberries
1 pound seedless grapes
2 apples, cored and sliced
2 peaches, sliced
1 avocado, sliced and peeled
1 cup granola
1 cup almonds, cashews, or
pecans
½ cup sesame seeds
½ cup sunflower seeds
½ cup shredded coconut
1 orange, peeled and
sectioned

DRESSING:
1 cup plain yogurt or sour
cream
Juice of 1 lemon
2 tablespoons honey
1 teaspoon ginger
1 teaspoon cinnamon

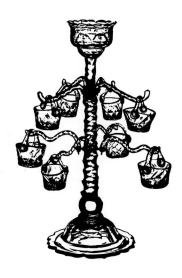

Cut glass and silver sweetmeat stand with baskets, 1765-85

CELERY SEED DRESSING

Preparation: 10 minutes

Add first 4 ingredients to blender or small mixing bowl. Slowly add part of vinegar, mixing or blending at medium speed. Add the rest of the vinegar and oil, beating until creamy. Add celery seed.

1/3 cup sugar
1 teaspoon dry mustard
1 teaspoon salt
1 small onion, minced
1/3 cup white vinegar
1 cup oil
1 tablespoon celery seed

Elizabeth Tufts Brown

SUMMER FRUIT DRESSING

Yield: Syrup for 8-10 cups fruit
Cooking: 15 minutes

In a heavy saucepan, slowly cook the water and sugar over low heat until the sugar has dissolved. When every granule of sugar is dissolved, raise the heat to medium high, and boil the mixture for 2 minutes. Pour in the citrus juices and continue to boil 4 minutes longer. Add Cointreau and Grand Marnier and boil another 4 minutes. Cool the syrup completely and store in tightly closed jars in refrigerator until needed (up to 3 weeks). Use to marinate any combination of fresh summer fruits.

1 cup water
¾ cup granulated sugar
Juice of 1 lemon, strained
Juice of 1 orange, strained
¼ cup Cointreau
3 tablespoons Grand Marnier or creme de cassis

Dena N. Forster

BLUE CHEESE DRESSING

Preparation: 5 minutes

Mix sour cream and mayonnaise. Pour Worcestershire sauce over it to cover. Add cheese, and salt and pepper to taste.

1 pint sour cream
1 tablespoon mayonnaise
2-3 tablespoons Worcestershire sauce
Salt and pepper
4 ounces crumbled blue cheese

POPPY SEED DRESSING

Yield: 1 pint
Preparation: 15 minutes

Mix sugar, mustard and salt and put in blender. Add vinegar. Add oil slowly while blending. Add poppy seed and onion. Blend a few seconds. Pour into a covered jar. Store in refrigerator. It will keep well for several weeks.

½ cup sugar
1 teaspoon dry mustard
1 teaspoon salt
½ cup vinegar
1 cup oil
4 teaspoons poppy seed
1 tablespoon onion, grated (optional)

"Good for any fruit salad—especially delicious on salads containing citrus fruits."
    Lydia T. Thomen

LEMON AND CHEESE SALAD DRESSING

Yield: 2 cups
Preparation: 5-10 minutes

Mix ingredients in order given. Pour into bottle or cruet and shake well. Serve at room temperature.

1 cup salad oil
2 tablespoons dry minced onions
½ teaspoon monosodium glutamate
2/3 cup lemon juice
¼ cup grated Parmesan cheese
3 tablespoons sugar
2 tablespoons water
Salt and pepper to taste

Lucie Frederick

CLASSIC VINAIGRETTE

Yield: 3 cups

Mix mustard and vinegar well; add sugar, olive oil, salt, and pepper. Pour into bottle. Shake well before using.

2 ounces Colman's dry mustard
6 ounces tarragon-flavored white wine vinegar
2 tablespoons sugar
17 ounces olive oil
Salt and pepper to taste

Emile Broglie

Blue-and-white wares were manufactured by Josiah Spode between 1781 and 1833 at Stoke-on-Trent, England. Spode's clientele for the wares included professionals and wealthy merchants who bought complete dinner services to use when entertaining.

In the late eighteenth to early nineteenth centuries, it was fashionable to take the Grand Tour of Europe. Consequently, many travel books were published, illustrated with engravings of the most spectacular sights. Such engravings became patterns for many potters, including Spode.

The earthenware egg stand, made between 1805 and 1820, is decorated with Spode's transfer-printed "Tiber" pattern. Named after the river shown in the foreground of the design, the pattern incorporates two aquatints from J. Merigot's book, *Views and Ruins in Rome and its Vicinity* (1798): "The Bridge and Castle of St. Angelo" and "Trajan's Column." St. Peter's is also visible beyond the bridge. Spode's manufacture of complete dinner services in this and three other Italian patterns from Merigot's book exemplifies the late eighteenth-century fascination with Roman ruins.

CLASSIC QUICHE

Serves: 3-4
Preparation: 30-40 minutes
Baking: 55 minutes
Freeze: Yes
Microwave: Yes

Preheat oven to 425°. Spread pie shell with butter. Fry bacon until crisp, drain on paper towels, and crumble. In small quantity of bacon fat, cook onion until tender. Spread bacon, onion, and cheese on bottom of pie shell. Beat eggs with hand beater, and add cream, salt, and nutmeg. Pour into shell. Bake 15 minutes; turn down to 325° and bake an additional 40 minutes or until knife inserted in center comes out clean. Remove from oven and let stand 10 minutes.

1 9-inch unbaked pie shell, well chilled
1 teaspoon butter
12 slices bacon, crumbled
¾ cup onion, chopped
¼ pound Swiss cheese, shredded (1 cup)
4 eggs
2 cups heavy cream
¾ teaspoon salt
Dash of nutmeg

"Use as an entree for luncheon or dinner with a salad, or cut into small portions for a first course."
    Debbie Kassner

CHEESE CASSEROLE PIE

Serves: 6-8
Baking: 1 hour

Remove the seeds from chilies and dice. In a large bowl, combine grated cheese and green chilies. Turn into a well-buttered 2-quart casserole. In a small bowl, with electric mixer at high speed, beat egg whites with a pinch of cream of tartar until peaks form. In a large bowl, combine egg yolks, milk, flour, salt and pepper and mix until thoroughly blended. Using a rubber spatula, fold beaten egg whites into egg yolk mixture. Pour egg mixture over cheese mixture in casserole. Using a fork gently "ooze" it through the cheese. Bake at 350° for 30 minutes. Remove from oven and arrange sliced tomatoes on top, overlapping around edge of casserole. Bake 30 minutes longer or until a knife inserted in center comes out clean. Garnish with a sprinkle of green chilies, if desired.

2 4-ounce cans green chilies, drained
1 pound Monterey Jack cheese, coarsely grated
4 eggs, separated
Pinch cream of tartar
2/3 cup canned evaporated milk, undiluted
1 tablespoon flour
½ teaspoon salt
⅛ teaspoon pepper
2 medium tomatoes, sliced

"Perfect with a steak and salad, served hot or cold."
    Mario Buatta

SMOKED SALMON QUICHE IN PATE BRISEE SHELL

Serves: 6
Preparation: 20 minutes
Baking: Approximately 1 hour

PASTRY SHELL:

Mix flour and salt in medium bowl, cutting in butter until mixture resembles fine crumbs. Mix egg yolk with 4 tablespoons ice water; add to flour mixture, stirring with fork until dough cleans sides of bowl. Add extra water if necessary. Shape dough into a ball; cover and refrigerate 30 minutes. Heat oven to 425°. Roll out dough and place into a pie plate or quiche pan with removable bottom. Prick bottom with fork. Line with foil and add dry beans to weight pastry. Bake for 10 minutes and remove from oven. Remove beans and foil. Cool on wire rack.

SALMON FILLING:

Mix eggs, half-and-half, cream, salt, pepper, and nutmeg in medium bowl; strain. Cut eight 5 x ¼-inch salmon strips. Reserve. Brush pastry shell with mustard, arranging remaining salmon over mustard. Sprinkle cheese over salmon. Pour custard on top but do not allow custard to spill over. Bake at 350° for 20 minutes. Remove from oven and arrange reserved salmon strips in a wheel design. Return to oven for 20 to 25 minutes more. Serve warm or cold.

Beverly Vermilyea

PASTRY SHELL:

1 1/3 cups flour
¼ teaspoon salt
6 tablespoons unsalted butter, cold
1 egg yolk
4-5 tablespoons ice water

SALMON FILLING:

5 eggs, lightly beaten
1½ cups half-and-half
1¼ cups heavy cream
¼ teaspoon salt
¼ teaspoon white pepper
Pinch of nutmeg
6 ounces smoked salmon, thinly sliced
1 teaspoon Dijon mustard
1½ cups grated Swiss cheese (6 ounces)

Salt-glazed stoneware jar, 1800-1900

ZUCCHINI QUICHE SUPREME

Serves: 4-6
Preparation: 30 minutes
Baking: 40-45 minutes

Prick crust and bake at 400° for about 8 minutes or until crust begins to turn golden. Remove from oven and cool. Wash and dry zucchini. Cut into ⅛-inch slices. Sauté zucchini in butter and add chives, salt, pepper, and oregano. Zucchini should retain its green color. Combine sour cream, eggs, and baking powder. Beginning with zucchini slices on bottom of crust, alternate layers of zucchini, sour cream mixture, and scattering of grated cheese. Continue layers, making two or more until all ingredients are used. Sprinkle Parmesan cheese and bread crumbs on top and sprinkle paprika or pepper over top for color. Bake at 325° for 40 to 45 minutes until puffy and golden. Serve hot or at room temperature.

1 9-inch deep dish pastry shell, unbaked
2 small zucchini (approximately 1 pound)
1 tablespoon butter
1½ tablespoons minced fresh chives
1 teaspoon salt
Black pepper
¼ teaspoon oregano
2 cups sour cream
2 large eggs, beaten
½ teaspoon baking powder
¾ cup Cheddar cheese, grated
¼ cup Parmesan or Romano cheese, grated
Seasoned bread crumbs
Paprika and/or cayenne pepper

Catherine H. Maxwell

QUICHE AUX FRUITS DE MER

Serves: 4-6
Preparation: 15 minutes
Baking: 30 minutes

Preheat oven to 375°. Cook onions in butter for 1 to 2 minutes over moderate heat until tender but not browned. Add shrimp and stir gently for 2 minutes. Sprinkle with salt and pepper. Add wine. Increase heat and boil for 1 minute. Allow to cool slightly. Beat eggs in bowl with cream, tomato paste, salt, and pepper. Blend in shrimp; taste for seasoning. Pour mixture into partially cooked pastry shell. Sprinkle with cheese. Bake in upper third of preheated oven for 25 to 30 minutes until quiche is puffed and browned.

2 tablespoons minced shallots or green onions
3 tablespoons butter
¼ pound (1 cup) shrimp, cooked and cut into small pieces
¼ teaspoon salt
Pinch pepper
2 tablespoons dry white wine
3 eggs
1 cup whipping cream
1 tablespoon tomato paste
¼ teaspoon salt
¼ teaspoon pepper
8-inch pastry shell, partially cooked
¼ cup grated Swiss cheese

Anne Beckley Coleman

SAUSAGE STRATA

Serves: 6-8
Preparation: 30 minutes (plus 12 hours refrigeration)
Baking: 45 minutes
Freeze: Yes

Cook sausage, drain well, and pat between paper towels. Beat eggs, milk, and mustard. Spread the bread cubes in bottom of well-greased 9 x 13-inch baking pan. Spread the sausage on top. Pour egg mixture over all and cover with grated cheese. Cover with plastic wrap and place in refrigerator overnight. Bake at 350° for 45 minutes. Serve with sweet rolls, orange juice, and fresh fruit.

1 pound bulk sausage
6 eggs
2 cups milk
1 teaspoon dry mustard
6-7 slices white bread, cubed (if desired remove crusts and butter before cubing)
1 cup grated sharp Cheddar cheese

"This is especially nice for brunch. The secret to success is to prepare it the day before."
  Patti Bullen

CHEESE AND GARLIC GRITS CASSEROLE

Serves: 4-8
Preparation: 30 minutes
Cooking: 20 minutes

Prepare grits according to package instructions. Fold in butter, grated cheese, Worcestershire sauce, Tabasco sauce, and garlic. Beat egg whites to form stiff peaks, and fold into grits. Pour into casserole dish. Bake at 400° for 20 minutes until lightly browned.

1 cup grits
¼ pound butter, melted
¾ pound Cheddar or American cheese, grated
1½ teaspoons Worcestershire sauce
Tabasco sauce
½-1 clove garlic, minced
2 egg whites, stiffly beaten

"Deemed delicious even by non-lovers of grits."
  Joyce Hill Stoner

Earthenware egg cup, 1800-1815

CRAB FRITTATA

Serves: 2-4
Preparation: 20 minutes
Cooking: 20 minutes

Sauté vegetables in butter; add salt and pepper. Cook covered for 5 to 7 minutes. Meanwhile, beat together eggs, milk and cheese. Combine crab, vegetables, and egg mixture in buttered casserole. Sprinkle with parsley. Bake at 350° for 20 minutes or until firm.

1 clove garlic, mashed
2/3 cup chopped onion
1 cup chopped zucchini
½ cup sliced mushrooms
2 tablespoons butter
1½ teaspoons salt
¼ teaspoon pepper
3 eggs
½ cup non-fat milk
½ cup grated Parmesan cheese
1 can crab meat, drained
Parsley

"Good for brunch or a light supper."
Elizabeth Tufts Brown

EGGS BENEDICT

Serves: 4-8
Preparation: 5 minutes
Cooking: 15 minutes

EGGS:
Toast English muffin halves, butter and cover each half with slice of bacon or ham. Poach eggs and place on top of meat. Top with Hollandaise Sauce.

HOLLANDAISE SAUCE:
Beat egg yolks in top of double boiler. Add melted butter very slowly while beating with whisk. Beat in lemon juice until thick. Remove from heat and serve immediately. Alternate method: Mix egg yolks and lemon juice in blender. Slowly pour in butter while mixing on low speed.

Mrs. Edgar Tufts

EGGS:
4 English muffins, split
8 slices Canadian bacon or boiled ham
8 eggs

HOLLANDAISE SAUCE:
3 egg yolks
½ cup melted butter
2 tablespoons lemon juice

POACHED EGGS WITH MORNAY SAUCE

Serves: 2-4

POACHED EGGS:
Fill a 2-quart saucepan with about 5-inches (¾ full) of water. Add cider vinegar and bring to a gentle boil. Break an egg in a cup while the water is boiling and gently pour the egg close to the surface. The water must be kept boiling or simmering. Add 3 more eggs in the same manner and let poach 2½ to 3 minutes until the whites are set. Remove the eggs with a perforated spoon and place them in cold water. When cool, remove the outside adherences on each egg and return eggs to the cold water until the time to be used.

POACHED EGGS:
Water
2 tablespoons cider vinegar
4 eggs

MORNAY SAUCE:
Melt 2 tablespoons of sweet butter in a saucepan. Add flour and mix well with wooden spoon. Cook for 1 to 2 minutes but do not let it brown. Bring milk to boil. Gradually add the boiling milk, salt, and onion to flour mixture. Cook for 10 minutes and then pass through a cheesecloth. Replace the sauce in the saucepan and add the yolks that have been mixed well with the cream. Add 1 tablespoon of sweet butter and tablespoon of Parmesan cheese. Place eggs in a shallow gratin dish. Pour the sauce over the eggs, sprinkle with grated Swiss cheese, and brown under the broiler.

MORNAY SAUCE:
3 tablespoons sweet butter
2 tablespoons flour
1 1/3 cups milk
Pinch of salt
1 small onion, sliced
2 egg yolks
¼ cup cream
1 tablespoon grated Parmesan cheese
1 tablespoon grated Swiss cheese

Winterthur Archives

CRAB QUICHE

Serves: 10-12
Preparation: 15 minutes
Cooking: 45 minutes

Combine mayonnaise, flour, eggs and milk. Mix until blended. Stir in crab\meat, cheese and onions. Pour into pastry lined 9-inch pie plate or quiche pan. Bake at 350° for 40 to 45 minutes.

½ cup mayonnaise
2 tablespoons flour
2 eggs, beaten
½ cup milk
1 2/3 cup canned crab meat
8 ounces Swiss cheese, diced
1/3 cup sliced green onions
Pastry pie shell

Betsy L. Smith

CHEESE PATTIES

Serves: 4-6
Preparation: 20 minutes
Cooking: 40 minutes

CHEESE PATTIES:
Combine all ingredients, except shortening, in order listed. Shape mixture to look like meat chops. Fry in hot shortening over low heat until golden brown on both sides. Serve with Creole Sauce.

CHEESE PATTIES:
1 pound coarsely shredded American cheese
4 tablespoons butter, softened
1 tablespoon Dijon mustard
1/8 teaspoon pepper
1 teaspoon salt
1 tablespoon finely chopped parsley or chives, or both
2 eggs, beaten
1 2/3 cups cracker crumbs
4-6 tablespoons shortening

CREOLE SAUCE:
Brown onion and green pepper in hot oil. Add other ingredients; bring to boiling point. Simmer for 20 minutes.

CREOLE SAUCE:
1/2 cup chopped onion
1/4 cup chopped green pepper
2 tablespoons vegetable oil
1 1/2 cups canned tomatoes
2 tablespoons chopped pimento
2 tablespoons sugar
1/2 teaspoon salt
Dash cayenne pepper
1 tablespoon vinegar
1 tablespoon ketchup
1 tablespoon Worcestershire sauce

Beverley Brainard Fleming

Butter churn, 1770-1840

STUFFED CHEESE WITH TEX-MEX DIP

Baking: 10 minutes

If cheese has a wax coating or rind, remove with a vegetable peeler and discard. If cheese is rounded, cut a thin slice from top of cheese and invert. Cheese should be able to stand on a flat surface. Use a spoon to hollow out the cheese; leave a shell about ½-inch thick. Reserve and crumble cheese bits. If using a rectangular piece of cheese, prepare the brick in same way.

In a saucepan combine the refried beans, jalapenos, tomato, garlic, oregano and Tabasco sauce. Simmer just until mixture is heated through. Taste for seasoning.

Line ovenproof dish with tortillas. Put hollowed-out cheese on top. Spoon heated mixture into cheese. Spread reserved crumbled cheese over filling. Dish may be refrigerated at this point.

Bake uncovered in preheated 350° oven for about 10 minutes or just until sides of cheese begin to melt. Serve immediately with corn chips.

Beverley Brainard Fleming

1 2-pound round of Fontina,
   Gouda or Provolone cheese
1 15-ounce can refried beans
1 4-ounce can jalapenos,
   chopped
1 medium tomato, peeled,
   seeded, and chopped
1 clove garlic, minced
¼ teaspoon dried oregano
¼ teaspoon Tabasco sauce
Vegetable oil (optional)
Tortillas
Corn chips

SUPER WHOLE-EGG CHEESE SOUFFLE

Serves: 6
Preparation: 15 minutes
Baking: 30-35 minutes

Do not separate eggs. Beat until thick and light. Mix in cream, salt, pepper and nutmeg. Beat well. Fold in cheeses. Pour into well-buttered 1½-quart soufflé or baking dish or an ovenproof 10½-inch frying pan. Bake at 425° for 30 to 35 minutes or until set. Recipe may be doubled or tripled for a large party.

6 eggs
1 cup heavy cream
1 teaspoon salt
Freshly ground pepper to taste
¼ teaspoon ground nutmeg
1½ cups grated Swiss or
   Cheddar cheese
½ cup grated Parmesan
   cheese

"Quick and easy. Especially nice with a green salad of lettuce and fresh herbs."
   Susan Cocks Small

Breads

In the eighteenth century, bread was baked weekly. The housewife heated her fireplace oven with a hardwood fire, spreading the coals to heat the oven evenly. After sweeping out the coals, she tested the temperature by thrusting her bare arm into the oven or by sprinkling flour in the oven to see if it scorched.

Breadstuffs are a main feature in most eighteenth-century cookbooks, probably because housewives and servants were expected to know how to cook the main dishes without the aid of a book. But even the bread recipes often only listed ingredients without measurements or instructions. The housewife learned from experience how to knead bread, how long to let it rise, whether the loaf could be placed directly on the bricks or should be put in a pan, and how long to bake it.

Winterthur's Kershner Kitchen came from a Pennsylvania German stone farmhouse built around 1755 in Berks County, Pennsylvania. Breads, cakes, and pies were favorites of the Pennsylvania German people. The Pennsylvania wrought-iron turner was made between 1775 and 1825 and was used to remove a loaf of bread from the oven in the great stone fireplace. The other iron tools shown were also used for cooking in the eighteenth and nineteenth centuries: a heart-shaped waffle iron, made in America, 1750-1820; an iron hanging kettle, made in America, 1790-1850; burl wood bowls and scoop, made in America, 1700-1800; an andiron made in America, 1725-75; a wrought-iron toaster with fleur-de-lis and heart motifs, made in America, 1750-1800; an iron and brass turner and ladle, made in America, 1760-1825; and an iron spider and trivet, made in America, 1725-1800.

DILL
BREAD

Yield: 2 loaves
Baking: 35-40 minutes
Freeze: Yes

Dissolve yeast in water. Add 2 teaspoons of sugar and set aside. Combine cottage cheese, onion, dill, baking powder, salt, sugar, and eggs. Add yeast mixture and mix. Add flour; knead. Put in greased bowl, turn, and cover. Let rise until doubled. Punch down; knead (no second rising). Form into 2 loaves and place in two greased 8 x 5 x 3-inch pans. Brush with melted butter and bake at 350° for 35 to 40 minutes.

2 packages dry yeast
½ cup warm water
2 teaspoons sugar
2 cups creamed cottage cheese
2 tablespoons dry onion
2 tablespoons dill weed
1 teaspoon baking powder
2 teaspoons salt
2 tablespoons sugar
2 eggs
4 ½ cups flour
Melted butter

"This unusual bread is delicious hot, straight out of the oven."
Anne Beckley Coleman

HERB
BREAD

Yield: 2 round loaves
Preparation: 30 minutes
(plus 2 hours rising time)
Baking: 35 minutes

Combine hot milk, sugar, salt, oil, nutmeg, sage, and celery seed. Cool to lukewarm. Soften the yeast in warm water. Add to milk mixture and mix well. Add eggs and 3 cups of flour, beating until smooth. Continue adding flour to make moderately soft dough. Turn out onto floured surface and knead until smooth and elastic, approximately 5 minutes. Place dough in oiled bowl, cover, and let rise in warm place until doubled in bulk, approximately 1 hour. Punch down, cover, and let rise 10 to 15 minutes. Shape into two equal rounds and place in 9-inch pie pans. Cover and let rise until doubled in bulk (45 to 60 minutes). Bake in preheated 400° oven for 35 minutes or until done. Cover loosely with aluminum foil for last ten minutes of the 35 minutes to prevent tops from burning.

2 cups milk, scalded
¼ cup sugar
1 tablespoon salt
¼ cup vegetable oil
1 teaspoon nutmeg
2 teaspoons sage
¼ cup celery seed
2 packages dry yeast
½ cup warm water
2 eggs
6-7 cups unbleached white flour

"Ideal sandwich bread; great toasted."
Ellen and Bert Denker

CHEESE BREAD

Yield: 2 loaves
Preparation: 3 hours (including rising time)
Baking: 40 minutes
Freeze: Yes

Mix 2½ cups of flour, sugar, salt, and yeast in a large bowl. Mix water and milk and heat in a saucepan until very warm. Gradually add liquid to dry ingredients and beat with electric mixer 2 minutes at medium speed, scraping bowl occasionally. Add ½ cup of flour and cheese. Beat for 2 minutes. Add enough flour to make a stiff dough. After turning out onto a floured board, knead until smooth and elastic, about 8-10 minutes. Place in a greased bowl; turn to grease top. Cover, place in a warm draft-free place, and let rise about 1 hour or until doubled in bulk. Punch dough down, turn onto board, cover, and let rise 15 minutes. Divide dough into two. Roll out each half to a 9 x 14-inch rectangle. Roll up, beginning with a short side. With seam side down, seal ends with fingers and fold under. Place in a 9 x 5-inch loaf pan in a warm draft-free place and let rise about 1 hour or until double. Bake at 375° on a low rack for about 40 minutes. Remove 1 loaf and tap sides and bottom; if it sounds hollow, the loaves are done. Remove from pans and cool on rack. Brush tops with melted butter.

Catherine H. Maxwell

8 cups unsifted flour
½ cup sugar
1 tablespoon salt
2 packages dry yeast
2 cups water
2/3 cup milk
¾ pound sharp Cheddar cheese, grated (3 cups)
Melted butter

CORNMEAL GEMS

Yield: 12 muffins
Preparation: 15 minutes
Baking: 20-25 minutes
Freeze: Yes

Mix and sift dry ingredients. Add milk gradually, then add eggs and butter. Dredge raisins in flour and add to the rest of the ingredients. Bake at 400° in greased muffin tins for 20 to 25 minutes.

Isabelle H. Bow

½ cup cornmeal
1 cup flour
3 teaspoons baking powder
6 tablespoons sugar
1 teaspoon salt
1 cup milk
2 eggs, well beaten
2 tablespoons butter, melted
1 cup raisins
1 tablespoon flour

ONION SHORTBREAD

Serves: 9
Preparation: 20 minutes
Cooking: 25-30 minutes

Preheat oven to 425°. Sauté onion in butter. Set aside. Combine muffin mix, egg, milk, corn and Tabasco sauce. Pour into buttered 8-inch square pan. Combine sour cream, salt, dill and ½ cup cheese with onions. Spread over batter. Sprinkle top with remaining cheese. Bake at 425° for 25 to 30 minutes. Serve warm.

1 large Spanish onion, sliced
¼ cup butter
12 ounces corn muffin mix
1 egg, beaten
1/3 cup milk
1 17-ounce can cream-style corn
2 drops Tabasco sauce
1 cup sour cream
¼ teaspoon salt
¼ teaspoon dill seed
1 cup grated sharp Cheddar cheese

Sandra Hounold

PARKER HOUSE MUFFINS

Yield: 12 muffins
Preparation: 15 minutes
Baking: 30 minutes

On low mixer speed cream butter and sugar until fluffy. Add eggs one at a time and mix until blended. Sift dry ingredients and add alternately with milk. Add vanilla. Mash ½ cup berries and stir in by hand. Fold in rest of berries. Butter muffin tins well (including top surface). Pile mixture high in cups and sprinkle with sugar. Bake at 375° for 30 minutes.

½ cup butter
1 cup sugar
2 eggs
2 cups flour
2 teaspoons baking powder
½ teaspoon salt
½ cup milk
1 teaspoon vanilla
2 ½ cups blueberries or cranberries
Raisins (optional)
2 teaspoons sugar (for topping)

Russell Ward Nadeau

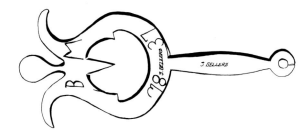

Wrought iron trivet, 1837

RUSSIAN BLACK BREAD

Yield: 2 round loaves
Preparation: 3 hours
Baking: 50 minutes

Combine unsifted flours. In a large bowl, mix thoroughly, 2 1/3 cups flour mixture, sugar, salt, coffee powder, onion powder, fennel seed, caraway seed, cereal, and undissolved yeast. Combine water, vinegar, molasses, chocolate, and butter in a saucepan. Heat over low heat until liquids are very warm (120°-130° F.). Solids do not need to melt. Slowly add to flour mixture and beat 2 minutes at medium speed of electric mixer. Add ½ cup of remaining flour mixture. Beat for 2 minutes at high speed, scraping sides of bowl occasionally. Add enough additional flour mixture to make a soft dough.

Turn onto lightly floured board. Cover; let rest 15 minutes. Knead until smooth and elastic, approximately 10 to 15 minutes (dough may be sticky). Place in a greased bowl, turning dough to grease top. Cover; let rise in warm place until doubled in bulk, approximately 1 hour.

Punch dough down. Turn onto lightly floured board and divide in half. Shape each half into a ball 5 inches in diameter. Place each ball in the center of a greased 9-inch round cake pan. Cover; let rise in warm place until doubled in bulk, approximately 1 hour.

Bake at 350° for 45 to 50 minutes. Meanwhile, combine cornstarch and cold water; cook over medium heat, stirring constantly, until mixture starts to boil. Continue cooking for 1 minute, stirring constantly. When bread is baked completely, brush cornstarch mixture on top of each loaf. Return to oven and bake 2 to 3 minutes, or until glaze sets. Remove from pans and cool on racks.

3 cups white flour
4 cups rye flour
1 teaspoon sugar
2 teaspoons salt
2 teaspoons instant coffee powder
2 teaspoons onion powder
½ teaspoon fennel seed, crushed
2 tablespoons caraway seed, crushed
2 cups whole bran cereal
2 packets dry yeast
2½ cups water
¼ cup vinegar
¼ cup dark molasses
1 ounce unsweetened chocolate
¼ cup butter
1 teaspoon cornstarch
½ cup cold water

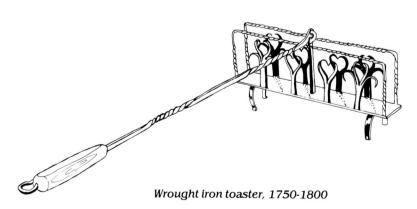

Wrought iron toaster, 1750-1800

MARYLAND BEATEN BISCUITS

Preparation: 30 minutes
Baking: 15 minutes

Sift flour and salt; cut in shortening. Add water a little at time. Dough should be very stiff. Beat on a breadboard with a wooden mallet until the dough blisters, approximately 20 minutes. Turn dough over and over while beating. Shape into balls about 1½ inches in diameter working with hands until satin smooth. Place on baking sheet and prick top of biscuits with fork. Bake at 500° for 15 minutes.

7 cups flour
1 teaspoon salt
1 cup shortening or lard
Water to make a stiff dough

Mrs. Harry Wallace, Jr.

BEER BREAD

Yield: 1 loaf
Preparation: 15 minutes
Baking: 1 hour

Mix all ingredients. Pour into greased loaf pan. Bake at 350° for 1 hour. Brush top immediately with melted butter.

3 cups self-rising flour
2 tablespoons sugar
12-ounces beer
Melted butter

"A good bread to accompany hearty winter stews."
    Elizabeth Tufts Brown

PARTY BISCUITS

Yield: 75 biscuits
Preparation: 50 minutes
Baking: 15 minutes

Sift together flour, salt, baking powder, and baking soda. Cut in shortening until mixture is the texture of large grains of sand. Pour buttermilk into flour mixture and mix quickly until all flour is moistened. Press into ball. Place on floured surface and knead. Roll out dough to ¼-inch thickness. Cut into 1½-inch biscuits. Place on baking sheet and bake at 450° for 15 minutes.

2 ½ cups flour
1 teaspoon salt
1 ½ teaspoons baking powder
½ teaspoon baking soda
**6 heaping tablespoons
    shortening**
1 cup buttermilk

"These are especially nice with thin slices of Smithfield ham. Place ham in biscuits, wrap in foil, and reheat in moderate oven for 10 minutes. Serve at once."
    Margaret Grayson Rowlett

WHEAT GERM HAMBURGER BUNS

Yield: 12 rolls
Baking: 15-20 minutes

In a saucepan scald milk. Add butter, honey and salt. Let cool until lukewarm. In a large bowl dissolve the yeast in ½ cup warm water with the sugar. When yeast mixture is bubbling add the cooled milk mixture, eggs and 3 cups of the flour. Beat with an electric mixer 2 minutes. Stir in the wheat germ. Gradually add the rest of the flour until the dough leaves the sides of the bowl. Turn onto a floured board and knead about 10 minutes. Put dough into a large greased bowl and turn so it is coated on all sides. Cover with a damp cloth until doubled. Punch down a few times to press out all the bubbles. Turn out onto a floured board and divide into twelve parts. Cover with a cloth and let rest about 10 to 15 minutes. Form each piece into a ball and put onto a greased baking sheet. Flatten a bit, brush tops with melted butter, cover and let rise until not quite doubled. Bake at 400° for 15 to 20 minutes. When done slice through center to use as hamburger bun or as individual dinner rolls. Can also be made into a loaf.

1 ½ cups milk
4 tablespoons butter or light oil
1-2 tablespoons honey
2 teaspoons salt
1 tablespoon plus 1 teaspoon dry yeast
½ cup warm water
½ teaspoon sugar
2 eggs
6 cups unbleached white flour
¾ cup wheat germ

Regina Smith

REFRIGERATOR ROLLS

Yield: 48-60 rolls
Preparation: 40 minutes
(plus 2 hours rising time)
Baking: 15 minutes
Freeze: Yes

Dissolve yeast in lukewarm water. Add shortening, sugar, salt, and potatoes to scalded milk. When cold, add yeast dissolved in water. Mix thoroughly and add eggs. Stir in enough flour to make a stiff dough. Knead well on a lightly floured surface. Place in large bowl, rub shortening over dough, and refrigerate. This recipe will keep for a week but is best on the second or third day. Before baking, let rise for 2 hours. Shape into desired size and bake at 425° for 15 minutes.

1 cake yeast or 1 package dry yeast
½ cup lukewarm water
2/3 cup shortening
½ cup sugar
1 teaspoon salt
1 cup mashed potatoes
1 cup milk, scalded
2 eggs, well beaten
7 cups flour

"Light and delicious."
Virginia S. Baldwin

DAVID EYRE'S PANCAKES

Serves: 4-6
Baking: 15-20 minutes

Preheat oven to 450°. Combine flour, milk, eggs, and nutmeg. Beat lightly (batter should be lumpy). On top of stove, melt 4 tablespoons of butter in 9-inch iron skillet. When butter is hot—not browned—pour batter into skillet. Place pan in oven and reduce heat to 425°. Bake 15 to 20 minutes until pancake has risen and browned. Serve in pan. Cut into wedges, sprinkle lightly with lemon juice and confectioners' sugar, and garnish with lemon slices.

½ cup flour
½ cup milk
2 eggs, lightly beaten
⅛ teaspoon nutmeg
4 tablespoons butter
Confectioners' sugar
1 lemon, sliced

"The blend of lemon and sugar makes the flavor heavenly. Honey or jam may also be used."
  Beverley Brainard Fleming

BANANA NUT BREAD

Yield: 1 loaf
Preparation: 15 minutes
Baking: 1 hour
Freeze: Yes

Mix ingredients in order given, sifting dry ingredients together before mixing. Pour into greased 9 x 5 x 2 ¾-inch pan. Bake at 350° for 1 hour or until done.

4 ripe bananas, mashed
1 cup sugar
Pinch of salt
1 egg
1 teaspoon baking powder
1 teaspoon baking soda
¼ teaspoon nutmeg
1 ½ cups flour
1/3 cup melted butter
1 teaspoon vanilla
1 ½ cups chopped walnuts

"This bread is moister than most; good banana flavor."
  Lucie Frederick

Salt-glazed stoneware jar, 1800-1900

COFFEE CAKE

Serves: 10
Preparation: 15 minutes
Baking: 45 minutes
Freeze: Yes

Mix first 8 ingredients in order given, mixing in eggs with a wooden spoon. Put half of batter in well-greased 10-inch tube pan. Mix nuts, sugar, and cinnamon and add to top of batter. Chopped apple or blueberries may be added. Put remaining batter in pan. Swirl mixture with spoon. Bake at 375° for 45 minutes.

¼ pound butter
1 cup sugar
1 teaspoon vanilla
2 eggs
2 teaspoons baking powder
1 teaspoon baking soda
1 cup sour cream
2 cups flour
½ cup chopped nuts
½ cup sugar
1 teaspoon cinnamon
½ cup chopped apple or blueberries (optional)

Suzanne C. Hamilton

LEMON LOAF

Yield: 1 loaf
Preparation: 10-15 minutes
Baking: 1 hour
Freeze: Yes

LOAF:
Cream butter, sugar, and eggs. Sift flour and baking powder. Add dry ingredients and lemon rind to butter mixture, alternating with milk. Add raisins or nuts, if desired. Bake for 1 hour at 350° in a well-greased and floured loaf pan.

LOAF:
½ cup butter
1 cup sugar
2 eggs
1 ½ cups flour
1 teaspoon baking powder
½ cup milk
1 lemon rind, grated
1 cup white raisins or ½ cup pecans (optional)

GLAZE:
While still warm, baste in two applications with the lemon juice and sugar mixture. Cool thoroughly before wrapping for freezer.

GLAZE:
Juice of 1 lemon
½ cup sugar

Mrs. Harry Wallace, Jr.

DELICATESSE DE MAIS-CREPES A LA MARYLAND

Serves: 3-4
Preparation: 8 minutes
Cooking: 1-2 minutes each

Sift cornmeal into a bowl; add salt and sugar. Mix or stir thoroughly after this and after each subsequent step. Scald the mixture with hot water barely under boiling point; add the water slowly, stirring the mixture well so that all parts come in contact with some of the hot water. This is critical. Stir in milk. Separate eggs and stir yolks into mixture; reserve whites. Melt shortening and stir into mixture. Beat the egg whites and fold into the mixture. Stir in baking powder. Bake on a very hot greased griddle. The crepes are baked on each side like griddle cakes. They should be 3½ to 4 inches in diameter and about 3/16-inch thick; the first side baked should be golden brown. The crepes should be buttered when served and may be eaten with honey, maple syrup, or jam.

Batter may be made the day before the first use. If this is done, the baking powder should not be added until shortly before it is to be used. Refrigerated batter will last several days. It should be taken out and left at room temperature for 30 minutes each time before it is used. If the batter is too thin the second or subsequent day, add an additional 1/3 teaspoon of baking powder. The crepes are light in consistency, but if properly scalded they are not difficult to turn or remove from the griddle.

The Honorable and Mrs. G. Burton Pearson, Jr.

1 cup white cornmeal
1 teaspoon salt
1 tablespoon sugar
¾ cup hot water
½ teaspoon cold whole milk
2 eggs, separated
1½ tablespoons shortening or butter
1 teaspoon baking powder
Shortening to grease griddle

BISHOP'S BREAD

Serves: 12
Preparation: 15 minutes
Baking: 30-40 minutes

To make sour milk, add 1 tablespoon vinegar to 1 cup milk. Mix butter, sugar, flour, cinnamon, and baking powder until crumbly. Set aside ½ cup for topping. Add remaining ingredients and mix well. Pour into buttered 8-inch square pan. Sprinkle topping over batter. Bake at 350° for 30 to 40 minutes, or until a toothpick inserted in the center comes out clean.

"Delightful for breakfast."
Patricia Campbell

1 cup milk, soured
½ cup butter
2 cups brown sugar
2½ cups flour
1 teaspoon cinnamon
1 teaspoon baking powder
1 egg, beaten
1 teaspoon salt
½ teaspoon baking soda

PUMPKIN SPICE BREAD

Yield: 2 loaves
Baking: 1 hour
Freeze: Yes

Grease and flour two 9 x 5 x 3-inch loaf pans. In large bowl, combine first 6 ingredients and set aside. Stir together pumpkin and oil. To this add eggs, one at a time, beating well after each addition. Make a well in the center of the flour mixture. Add pumpkin mixture; stir until flour is just moistened. Pour into prepared pans. Bake at 350° for 1 hour until cake tester inserted in center comes out clean. Cool in pan 10 minutes. Remove and cool on racks.

Ann Van Ogtrop

3 ½ cups unsifted flour
2 ½ cups sugar
2 teaspoons baking soda
1 ½ teaspoons salt
1 teaspoon cinnamon
1 teaspoon nutmeg
1 can (1 pound) pumpkin
1 cup corn oil
4 eggs

HOLIDAY PUMPKIN BREAD

Yield: One 8½ x 4½-inch loaf or two 7 ¼ x 3 ¼-inch loaves
Preparation: 30 minutes
Baking: 1 hour
Freeze: Yes

Cream shortening and stir in sugar and eggs. Stir in molasses and pumpkin. Sift together flour, baking powder, baking soda, salt, and spices. Add to pumpkin mixture. Beat until well blended. Add nuts and raisins. Pour mixture into well-greased loaf pans. Arrange walnuts on top and bake at 350° for 1 hour or until the center is done. Smaller loaves require less baking time; check periodically until done in the center. Serve with soft butter or cream cheese.

1/3 cup shortening
1 cup sugar
2 eggs
½ cup dark or light molasses
1 cup mashed pumpkin
2 cups flour
¼ teaspoon baking powder
1 teaspoon baking soda
½ teaspoon salt
2 teaspoons pumpkin pie spice (or 1 teaspoon cinnamon, ½ teaspoon each cloves and nutmeg)
1 cup chopped walnuts (optional)
½ cup raisins (optional)
Additional whole walnuts, top decoration (optional)

"Nice to have in the freezer to dress up an ordinary meal or as a last-minute house guest gift."
    Patti Bullen

KOLACHES

Yields: 2 dozen rolls
Baking: 15 minutes

DOUGH:
Scald milk in small saucepan; cool to lukewarm. Sprinkle yeast into very warm water in a large bowl. Stir until yeast dissolves.

Beat butter with sugar, salt and egg yolks until light and fluffy in large bowl with electric mixer. Stir in yeast mixture, cooled milk, and 2 cups of flour. Beat 5 minutes at medium speed or 300 strokes by hand.

Stir in remaining flour and make a very soft dough; cover with a damp towel. Let rise in a warm place, away from draft. 1 hour, or until doubled in bulk. Stir dough down; turn onto a lightly floured cloth or board. Flour hands; knead dough several minutes; divide in half.

Cut first half of dough into 12 even pieces; shape each into a smooth ball. Place balls 2 inches apart on a greased cookie sheet; cover with cloth. Do the same with the second half. Let all rise again 45 minutes or until doubled in bulk. Press large hollows in center of round rolls with fingertips; place tablespoonful of prune filling in each.

Bake in moderate oven (350°) 15 minutes or until golden brown. Remove from cookie sheet and cool on wire racks.

PRUNE FILLING:
Chop prunes and combine with water and sugar in a medium saucepan. Cook slowly, 15 minutes or until thick, stirring constantly. Cool. Stir in grated orange rind. Makes 1¾ cups.

DOUGH:
½ cup milk
2 envelopes active dry yeast
½ cup very warm water
¾ cup butter
½ cup sugar
1 teaspoon salt
4 egg yolks
4½ cups sifted flour

PRUNE FILLING:
12 ounces prunes, pitted
2 cups water
2 tablespoons sugar
2 teaspoons grated orange rind

OATMEAL RIBBON LOAF

Yield: 1 loaf
Preparation: 15 minutes
Baking: 40-50 minutes

Mix first 6 ingredients; stir in oatmeal and egg and beat well. Melt and cool shortening; add to mixture. Combine orange juice and water and add to batter, mixing well. Pour half of batter into a loaf pan, sprinkle with raisins, then pour in remainder of batter. Bake at 350° for 40 to 50 minutes.

Mrs. Robert S. Chapin

1½ cups flour
½ cup sugar
2 teaspoons baking powder
½ teaspoon baking soda
½ teaspoon salt
1 teaspoon cinnamon
1 cup oatmeal
1 egg
2 tablespoons shortening
2/3 cup orange juice
1/3 cup water
1 cup raisins

OATMEAL FRUIT MUFFINS

Yield: 12 muffins
Preparation: 15 minutes
Baking: 20-25 minutes
Freeze: Yes

In a large bowl, combine first 7 ingredients. In a small bowl, beat remaining ingredients. Pour liquid mixture into flour mixture and stir just until moistened (the batter will be lumpy). Divide into 12 greased muffin tins. Bake at 400° for 20 to 25 minutes.

1¼ cups flour
1 cup rolled oats
½ cup dried fruit, chopped
¼ cup dark brown sugar
3 teaspoons baking powder
¾ teaspoon cinnamon
½ teaspoon salt
1 cup milk
¼ cup oil
1 egg

Isabelle H. Bow

SWEDISH PANCAKES

Serves: 2
Preparation: 15 minutes

Beat egg whites until stiff but not dry. In another bowl, beat egg yolks and add milk, flour, sugar, salt and baking powder. Mix well. Mixture should be the consistency of heavy cream. Fold in egg whites. Drop on hot griddle and cook both sides to desired color.

2 eggs, separated
½ cup milk
1/3 cup flour
1½ teaspoons sugar
½ teaspoon salt
½ teaspoon baking powder

Vera Anderson

APPLE CHEESE WALNUT BREAD

Yield: 1 loaf
Preparation: 15 minutes
Baking: 1 hour

Cream butter; add sugar and eggs, one at a time. Sift flour, baking powder, soda, salt, and ginger. Add alternately with apples to butter mixture. Stir in cheese and walnuts. Spoon into buttered loaf pan. Bake at 350° for one hour. Allow to cool.

½ cup butter
¾ cup sugar
2 eggs
1¾ cups sifted flour
1 cup grated apples
1 teaspoon baking powder
½ teaspoon baking soda
½ teaspoon salt
¼ teaspoon ginger
½ cup grated Cheddar cheese
½ cup chopped walnuts
Raisins (optional)

Fish has been plentiful and popular in America since colonial times. In the late eighteenth century, senators and representatives in Washington, D.C., sailed down the Potomac River on Saturdays for shad-eating parties. In the nineteenth century the clambake was a popular social outing in New England. Clams, fish, potatoes, and corn were steamed by layering them with seaweed and enveloping them between hot rocks and a wet canvas.

Eighteenth-century recipe books included instructions for pickling, smoking, stuffing, and baking all kinds of fish. Boiled fish, however, was most popular because it was associated with French cuisine. Early eighteenth-century recipes called for boiling fish in salted water for one or two hours and serving it with a sauce of horseradish, lemon, and butter. Fish and shellfish were also stewed in white wine. By the mid-eighteenth century, tastes had changed and the cooking time for fish was shortened.

Baked Stuffed Sea Trout is served on a blue and white tin-glazed earthenware fish strainer made in Holland, 1720-60. A lemon-butter sauce is held in a tin-glazed earthenware sauceboat with semicircular handles in the form of foxes, probably made in Ireland. The silver sauce ladle was made by Shepherd and Boyd in Albany, New York, 1820-29. The fork and the knife with pistol-shaped porcelain handles and steel tines and blade were probably made in England, 1750-1875. The drop-leaf table of walnut, butternut, and pine is from New England, 1700-1725.

SALMON IN CRUST WITH HOLLANDAISE SAUCE

Serves: 6
Preparation: 5 hours (1 day before serving), plus 1 hour day of serving
Baking: 45 minutes

DOUGH:

Dough can be prepared several days in advance and frozen. It is preferable to prepare it at least 1 day before serving. Melt butter in saucepan with milk. Put 5 cups of the flour in a large bowl with salt, sugar, butter mixture, and eggs; blend. While mixture is still warm, add dissolved yeast. Beat 2 to 3 minutes then add the remaining flour. Continue to blend. Turn out onto a lightly floured board and let rest for 2 minutes, then knead for a minute or two. Place in a large bowl and cover with a damp towel. Let rise until tripled, about 3 hours. Turn out onto floured board and press with the palm of your hands; fold and repeat. Return to bowl and let rise again 1½ hours until doubled. Turn onto work surface and flatten. Place in bowl again; cover and refrigerate until chilled.

DOUGH:
- ½ **pound butter**
- ½ **cup milk**
- **7 cups flour**
- **1 teaspoon salt**
- **3 tablespoons sugar**
- **8 large eggs**
- **2 packages dry active yeast, dissolved in ½ cup warm water**

SALMON:

On a stiff piece of paper, draw an outline of the fish to use as a template. Rub outside of salmon with olive oil, then salt and pepper the inside. Chop dill and add with fennel seed to the cavity of the fish. Roll one-third of the dough out until it is approximately ⅛-inch thick. Use fish template and cut dough with a 1-inch excess edge. Place fish on dough and roll out another piece to cover. Press edges together and tuck under fish. Fashion fins and tail with remaining dough and use small scissors to lightly snip the dough and create scales. Brush with egg mixture. Bake at 400° for 45 minutes until internal temperature is 165° on a meat thermometer. Serve with Hollandaise Sauce.

SALMON:
- **3 pounds salmon, cleaned and scaled with head removed (any firm white fish may be substituted)**
- **Olive oil**
- **Salt**
- **Pepper**
- ½ **teaspoon fennel seed**
- ½ **cup fresh dill**
- **1 egg, beaten with 1 tablespoon water**

HOLLANDAISE SAUCE:

Place egg yolks in a double boiler with water just reaching top pot. As water begins to boil, start adding the pats of butter, stirring constantly. Keep simmering. As butter melts, continue adding all of butter. Keep stirring and as sauce begins to thicken, add lemon juice. If mixture becomes too thick, add 1 tablespoon of warm water at a time until you get desired consistency.

HOLLANDAISE SAUCE:
- **6 egg yolks**
- ½ **pound butter, cut into ½-inch pieces**
- **4 tablespoons lemon juice (or to taste)**

Regina Smith

OYSTERY SUPREME

Serves: 6
Preparation: 20-30 minutes

MAIN DISH:

Prepare Quick Hollandaise Sauce and keep warm. Toast muffin halves. Sauté bacon or ham and place on muffins. Sauté onions and spinach in butter until onions are tender; add nutmeg. Place ¼ cup spinach mixture on muffins. Keep warm. Simmer oysters in their own juice for 2 to 3 minutes, or until edges curl. Remove oysters with slotted spoon and place on top of spinach. Pour Quick Hollandaise Sauce on top, sprinkle with Parmesan cheese, and serve immediately.

QUICK HOLLANDAISE SAUCE:

Place egg yolks, lemon juice, and seasonings in blender. Blend for 5 seconds at low speed. Slowly pour in melted butter until sauce is thick and smooth. Keep warm. Makes ¾ cup of sauce.

Joy Hartshorn

MAIN DISH:

1 pint oysters
1 package frozen chopped spinach, thawed
1 tablespoon butter
2 tablespoons chopped onions
⅛ teaspoon nutmeg
6 thin slices Canadian bacon or ham
3 English muffins, split
Parmesan cheese

QUICK HOLLANDAISE SAUCE:

2 egg yolks
3 tablespoons lemon juice
¼ teaspoon salt
Dash cayenne pepper
½ cup butter, melted

CRAB IMPERIAL

Serves: 4
Preparation: 20-25 minutes
Baking: 10 minutes

Place crab meat in a large bowl. Brown onion in butter over medium low heat. Sprinkle flour over onion quickly; pour milk in gradually, stirring until thick. Mix in bread cubes. Add mayonnaise, salt, pepper, Worcestershire sauce, lemon juice, and horseradish. Mix together. Pour mixture over crab meat and mix well. Place in four individual dishes. Sprinkle with paprika. Broil until bubbly.

Debbie Kassner

1 pound "special" crab meat
1 tablespoon diced onion
1 tablespoon butter
1 tablespoon flour
½ cup milk
2 slices white bread, cubed
½ cup mayonnaise
Salt and pepper to taste
1 tablespoon Worcestershire sauce
1 tablespoon lemon juice
1 tablespoon horseradish
Paprika

CRAB AND SHRIMP SOUFFLE

Serves: 8
Preparation: 2 hours
Baking: 1¼ hours
Microwave: 35 minutes

Butter a 10-inch square casserole. Put in cubed bread. Mix crab meat, shrimp, mayonnaise, onion, pepper, celery, and mushroom soup and spread over bread. Beat eggs slightly before adding. Add milk to eggs, then pour over crab and bread mixture. Cover with foil and place in refrigerator for 24 hours. Bake at 325° for 15 minutes. Remove from oven and sprinkle with grated cheese and paprika. Return to oven and bake at 325° for 1 hour. Serve immediately. Microwave at medium high 30 to 34 minutes, rotating dish ¼ turn every 10 minutes until set but soft in center. Add cheese and paprika. Microwave at medium high 1 to 2 minutes until cheese is melted.

Ann Marie Keefer

8 slices white bread, cubed
2 cups crab meat
2 cups small shrimp
½ cup mayonnaise
1 cup chopped onion
1 green pepper, chopped
1 cup chopped celery
1 can cream of mushroom soup
4 eggs
3 cups milk
½ cup grated sharp cheese
Paprika

BUTTERFLY SHRIMP

Serves: 4-6
Preparation: 2 hours
Cooking: 20 minutes

FRIED SHRIMP:
Remove shells from shrimp, leaving tail sections attached. Devein and slit shrimp down the back, leaving the two sides attached. Add 2 teaspoons salt and baking soda and let stand at least 1 hour. Rinse and dry shrimp. To prepare batter, blend flour and water until smooth. Add 1 teaspoon salt and baking powder. Mix well until all lumps have disappeared. Dip shrimp into batter and fry in hot peanut oil until golden brown. Serve the shrimp with Hot Sauce.

HOT SAUCE:
To prepare sauce, heat oil in saucepan. Add ketchup and tomato paste, then add water, sugar, salt, vinegar, and soy sauce. As mixture begins to boil, add dissolved cornstarch, curry powder, and Tabasco sauce. Stir until thickened.

Eli Bauman

FRIED SHRIMP:
24 large shrimp
3 teaspoons salt
2 teaspoons baking soda
2 cups flour
2 cups water
4 teaspoons baking powder
Peanut or corn oil for deep frying

HOT SAUCE:
2 teaspoons oil
¼ cup ketchup
2 teaspoons tomato paste
2 cups water
4 heaping tablespoons sugar
1 teaspoon salt
6 tablespoons white vinegar
2 tablespoons light soy sauce
3 tablespoons cornstarch dissolved in 6 tablespoons water
½ teaspoon curry powder
5 dashes Tabasco sauce

OYSTER PIE VOL-AU-VENT

Serves: 6-8
Baking: 30-45 minutes

Fry bacon, drain, crumble, and set aside. Sauté in butter scallions, onions, green pepper, celery, and mushrooms. Add flour, then oysters and their liquor, cooking until thickened. Add remaining seasonings. If too thick, add chicken broth. Pour all into vol-au-vent shell. Bake at 400° for 30 to 45 minutes.

3 slices bacon
¼ pound butter
2 scallions with three inches of their green leaves, sliced thin
1 small onion, minced
½ green pepper, minced
1 small stalk celery, chopped
4 fresh mushrooms, chopped
3 tablespoons flour
4 dozen oysters (2 pints) in their liquor
3 tablespoons chopped fresh parsley
1 tablespoon lemon juice
¼ ounce cognac
1 cup chicken broth, if necessary to thin
¼ teaspoon cayenne pepper
Vol-au-vent pastry shell (two crusts)

"A vol-au-vent is a large baked patty shell that has a round hole cut in top of the crust to serve as a vent. It can be made by hand or purchased in fine pastry shops."
Eleanor Cleaver

PARTY OYSTERS

Serves: 5-6

Stew oysters in liquor until their edges curl; remove from heat. In a large skillet, sauté mushrooms in butter. When mushrooms are lightly done, sprinkle with flour, stirring to avoid burning. (Additional flour may be added later if mixture is too thin.) With a draining spoon, put oysters into mushrooms, adding liquor until desired consistency is reached, keeping temperature on low. Cream may be added to alter color if necessary. Add sherry, salt, and pepper. Place slices of ham on each piece of toast. Top with oysters in sauce.

Mrs. Charles W. Lyle

1 quart stewing oysters with liquor
1½ pounds fresh mushroom caps, sliced
Flour
1-2 ounces dry sherry
Salt and pepper
Thinly sliced Smithfield ham, enough for 6 servings
6 slices thin dry toast

OYSTERS MARDI GRAS

Serves: 4-6
Preparation: 15 minutes
Baking: 10-15 minutes

Place oysters in a casserole dish and sprinkle with onion and parsley. Put crumbs on top. Melt butter; add lemon juice, mustard, Worcestershire sauce and pour over crumbs. Bake at 450° until oysters curl, 10 to 15 minutes.

3 dozen oysters
2/3 cup parsley
2/3 cup green onions
1 cup bread crumbs
½ cup butter
1 small lemon
½ teaspoon mustard
2 teaspoon Worcestershire sauce

Mrs. J. Earl Blouin

SHRIMP REMOULADE

Yield: 1½ quarts
Preparation: 10 minutes
(plus 6 hours refrigeration)

Put eggs, paprika, salt, and mustard into mixing bowl. Slowly beat in oil. When thick add vinegar; squeeze in lemon juice and drop in lemon pieces. Add remaining ingredients through parsley. Refrigerate 6 hours; remove lemon pieces. Place shrimp on bed of lettuce and dress with rémoulade.

2 eggs
4 tablespoons paprika
2 teaspoons salt
½ cup creole mustard
1½ cups oil
½ cup vinegar
1 lemon, quartered
½ cup ketchup
3 bay leaves
2 teaspoons horseradish
3 cloves garlic
½ cup green onions
½ cup celery
¼-½ cup parsley
3-4 pounds shrimp, boiled and shelled
Lettuce

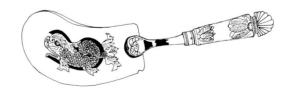

Silver fish knife, with mother-of-pearl handle, 1813-45

SHRIMP GIANNI
WITH FETA CHEESE

Serves: 4
Preparation: 20 minutes
Cooking: 45 minutes

Heat ½ cup of olive oil in large skillet over medium high heat until almost smoking. Add onion and sauté until translucent. Add tomatoes. Heat to boiling; reduce heat and simmer, covered, for five minutes. Stir in wine, celery, parsley, bay leaf, cumin, salt, and pepper. Simmer, covered, for 30 minutes. Sauté shrimp in shells in garlic and 2 tablespoons olive oil, until shrimp begin to curl. Remove and cool slightly. Remove shells. Stir shrimp into sauce during the last 5 minutes of cooking time. Crumble feta cheese over top. Serve with rice.

½ cup olive oil, plus 2 tablespoons
½ cup chopped onion
½ can Italian plum tomatoes, drained
1 cup white wine
½ cup finely chopped celery
½ cup snipped fresh parsley
1 bay leaf, crumbled
½ teaspoon cumin
Salt and pepper
1 pound fresh shrimp in shells
1 clove garlic, crushed
½ pound feta cheese

Beverly Vermilyea

SHRIMP
CURRY

Serves: 4
Cooking: 25 minutes

Sauté onions with garlic and butter. When golden brown, mix in curry powder, salt, and pepper. Add tomatoes, crushing them with a wooden spoon to release the juice. Add hot water and shrimp; simmer for 20 minutes.

2 onions, sliced
2 cloves garlic
4 tablespoons butter
½ tablespoon curry powder
Salt and pepper
½ pound tomatoes, quartered
2 tablespoons hot water
1 pound shrimp, cooked and shelled

Emile Broglie ℳ

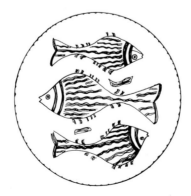

Red earthenware plate with sgraffito decoration, 1800-1825

SHRIMP AND SCALLOPS GRUYERE

Serves: 8-10
Preparation: 1 hour
Cooking: 30 minutes

Make a cream sauce in the top of a double boiler with ¾ cup of butter, flour, and milk. Cut the cheese into small pieces and add to the sauce. Stir until cheese melts. Add garlic powder, 2½ teaspoons of salt, pepper, mustard, tomato paste, and 2 teaspoons of the lemon juice. Poach scallops for 10 minutes in water to which the remaining 1 teaspoon lemon juice and ½ teaspoon of salt have been added. If cream sauce is too thick, add a little scallop broth. Drain scallops and add scallops and shrimp to the sauce. Sauté the mushrooms in the remaining 2 tablespoons of butter. Add to the sauce. Heat for 15 minutes. Sauté green pepper in a little butter and add to sauce. Put all in chafing dish. Serve with rice or patty shells.

¾ **cup plus 2 tablespoons butter**
¾ **cup flour**
3 cups milk
12 ounces Gruyère cheese
¼ **teaspoon garlic powder**
3 teaspoons salt
Pepper
¼ **teaspoon dry mustard**
2 teaspoons tomato paste
3 teaspoons lemon juice
1 pound raw scallops
1 pound shrimp, cooked and cleaned
½ **pound mushrooms, sliced**
3 tablespoons diced green pepper

"Delicious — worth the time spent in preparation. Sauce may be made ahead and the shrimp and scallops added on the serving day."
    Virginia S. Baldwin

SCALLOPS BEURRE POUR ESCARGOT

Serves: 4-6
Preparation: 20 minutes
Cooking: 2 minutes

Poach scallops in red wine to cover, seasoned with salt, thyme, 1 tablespoon parsley, 1 teaspoon shallots, and one clove garlic. Scallops will cook very quickly, approximately 1 to 2 minutes. Arrange scallops in individual ramekins or shells (they can be covered and refrigerated at this point.) Make beurre pour escargot by creaming the butter with the rest of the parsley, shallots, and garlic. Top each ramekin of scallops with a spoonful of the butter mixture. Put under broiler flame just long enough to brown them well on top.

2 pounds bay scallops
Red wine
1 teaspoon salt
½ **teaspoon thyme**
7 tablespoons finely chopped parsley
3-4 shallots, finely chopped
3-4 cloves garlic, finely chopped
¾ **cup butter**

"Serve as first course at dinner or main course at luncheon."
    Mary Ellen Smith

SEAFOOD AU GRATIN

Serves: 10-12
Preparation: 1 hour
Baking: 15-20 minutes

Break seafood into bite-sized pieces. Melt ½ cup butter in large saucepan. Add flour, blend, and cook over low heat stirring constantly for 1 minute. Add milk, tomato purée, salt, pepper, paprika, garlic, and cheeses. Cook, stirring constantly until cheese is melted and sauce is thick and bubbly. Add sherry and brandy. Combine seafood and sauce, stirring lightly to avoid breaking seafood pieces. Turn into 3-quart baking dish. Sprinkle with bread crumbs mixed with remaining 1 tablespoon of butter. Bake at 325° for 15 to 20 minutes. Seafood and sauce may be prepared in advance but should be refrigerated separately until cooking time. If seafood and sauce are cold, increase baking time to 30 minutes. Alternative: For a cream sauce, substitute ¾ cup heavy cream for tomato purée.

2 pounds lobster, cooked
2 pounds shrimp, cooked and shelled
1 pound crab meat, cooked
½ cup butter plus 1 tablespoon
½ cup flour
4 cups milk
¾ cup tomato puree
1 tablespoon salt
¼ teaspoon red pepper
¾ teaspoon paprika
1 clove garlic, minced
2 ounces Gruyère cheese, grated
1½ cups grated sharp Cheddar cheese
¼ cup sherry
¼ cup brandy
½ cup soft bread crumbs

Ursula H. Bright

THE ARTIST'S SHRIMP

Serves: 10
Preparation: 30 minutes
Cooking: 30 minutes

SHRIMP:
Bring water and pickling spices to boil in large pot (such as lobster pot). Add shrimp and boil 15 minutes. Drain and place shrimp with spices on large platter.

SAUCE:
Melt butter and add remaining ingredients. Serve hot in individual sauce dishes. Guests should peel their own shrimp and dip in sauce.

SHRIMP:
10 pounds jumbo shrimp
3 boxes pickling spices

SAUCE:
½ pound butter
½ cup Worcestershire sauce
1 cup ketchup
Salt
Pepper
Tabasco sauce
Celery salt

"Elegant but fun dinner. Nice served with salad of choice and baked potato skins."
Barbara Morris

SHRIMP MARIA STUART

Serves: 4-6
Preparation: 10 minutes
Cooking: 10-20 minutes

Sauté onion in butter until transparent. Add shrimp and stir. Add brandy, heat and ignite. When flame dies add lemon juice. Add cream, stirring gently. Add tomato paste, salt, pepper, parsley, and Worcestershire sauce. Simmer for a few minutes until blended. Serve with rice. Accompany with a chilled dry white wine.

1 onion, minced
½ cup butter
2 cups boiled shrimp, shelled and cleaned
½ cup brandy
Juice of 1 small lemon
1 cup heavy cream
4 tablespoons tomato paste or ketchup
Salt and freshly ground pepper
4 tablespoons chopped parsley
1 tablespoon Worcestershire sauce

"Great dish for a quick, pre-theatre supper."
    Mrs. Frank C. Springer, Jr.

COLD SEAFOOD SAUCE

Yield: 1½ quarts
Preparation: 15 minutes

Mix thoroughly and refrigerate.

1 pint mayonnaise
1 pint chili sauce
½ pint India relish, drained
1 hard-boiled egg, chopped
1 teaspoon chopped chives
1 teaspoon chopped onion
1 jar of pimento, chopped
1 teaspoon chopped celery
1 teaspoon prepared mustard
Salt, pepper, and paprika to taste

Nancy Corroon

Salt-glazed stoneware bowl with scratch blue decoration, 1745-70

SEAFOOD CELESTE

Serves: 5-6
Preparation: 30 minutes
Cooking: 15 minutes
Freeze: Yes

In saucepan melt butter over low heat, then stir in flour and seasonings. Cook and stir for a minute or two until well blended. Raise heat to medium and gradually add milk, continuing to stir until mixture is thickened and smooth. Add lemon juice to undrained clams, then add to milk mixture. Reheat to boiling and remove from heat. Place frozen shrimp in colander and thaw under cold running water. Press or squeeze out excess liquid. Add to mixture in saucepan and reheat slowly, stirring constantly until shrimp are heated through. Do not allow to boil. Serve over chow mein noodles.

4 tablespoons butter
5 tablespoons flour
¼ teaspoon marjoram
½ teaspoon paprika
⅛ teaspoon pepper
1½ cups milk or half-and-half
2 teaspoons lemon juice
1 6½-ounce can minced clams, undrained
6-8 ounces shrimp, cooked
1 5-ounce can chow mein noodles

Marian Blakeman

CHESAPEAKE BAY SEAFOOD SPECIAL

Serves: 4
Preparation: 30 minutes
Cooking: 30 minutes

Melt butter in frying pan. Sauté onions and garlic in butter for 5 minutes. Add scallops, crab meat, and all herbs. Pour wine over ingredients and simmer, covered, for 10 to 15 minutes, stirring occasionally. Add mushrooms and green pepper and simmer, covered, for 3 to 5 minutes, stirring occasionally. Remove from heat and serve.

¼ pound butter
2 onions, chopped
5 cloves garlic, chopped
1 pound sea scallops
1 pound claw crab meat
1 tablespoon parsley flakes
½ teaspoon sweet basil
¼ teaspoon tarragon
1 tablespoon curry
1 teaspoon thyme
1 pinch rosemary
2 dashes paprika
1 dash black pepper
2 bay leaves
1 cup dry white wine
1 cup diced mushrooms
1 green bell pepper, diced

Fred and Jane Drummond

FILLET OF
SOLE WITH BANANAS

Serves: 4
Preparation: 15 minutes
Cooking: 10 minutes

Roll fillets in flour, salt, pepper, and paprika. Melt butter in skillet and brown fillets 2 to 3 minutes on each side until golden brown and flaky. Remove to heated platter. Add to skillet sherry or white wine, ginger, lemon juice, brown sugar, and bananas, simmering 2 minutes. Pour sauce and bananas over fillets. Sprinkle with toasted almond slivers.

2-4 fillets of sole (or flounder)
Flour
Salt and pepper
Paprika
¼ cup butter
½ cup sherry or dry white wine
½ teaspoon ginger
2 tablespoons lemon juice
2 tablespoons brown sugar
2 bananas cut into quarters
lengthwise
½ cup almond slivers, toasted

"Good served with avocado and lettuce salad and garlic bread."
  Louise P. Cole

CRAB MEAT
CHANTILLY

Serves: 4
Preparation: 45 minutes

Thaw crab; drain and cut in chunks. Sauté onion in butter until tender, not brown. Stir in flour, salt, and cayenne. Add milk. Cook, stirring constantly until thickened. Remove from heat. Stir in salad dressing and fold in crab meat. Arrange asparagus in shallow 1½-quart baking dish. Cover with crab mixture; sprinkle with cheese. Broil about 4 inches from heat 3 to 5 minutes or until lightly browned and hot. Can be served on toast points.

6-7 ounces frozen or canned
king or snow crab
2 tablespoons chopped green
onion
2 tablespoons butter
1 tablespoon flour
½ teaspoon salt
Cayenne
1 cup half-and-half or milk
¼ cup Miracle Whip
10-ounces asparagus spears,
cooked and drained
1 tablespoon grated Parmesan
cheese

"Delicious for a special luncheon."
  Anna V. Harford

CRAB NEWBURG

Serves: 4
Cooking: 10-15 minutes

Melt butter in frying pan, adding the crab meat. Cook until meat begins to sizzle, stirring occasionally. Add cayenne and pour sherry over mixture, cooking 1 minute. Add ¾ cup cream and heat through. Add the beaten egg yolks with the 2 tablespoons of cream and stir very gently, without breaking the meat (if possible) and without boiling, until egg is smoothly cooked into the cream. Mushroom and pimento may be added, if desired. Serve with toast triangles.

1 pound crab meat
2 tablespoons butter
Dash of cayenne
2 tablespoons sherry
¾ cup plus 2 tablespoons light cream
2 egg yolks, well beaten
Chopped mushrooms and pimento (optional)

Maurice Gilliand

EASY LOBSTER NEWBURG

Serves: 4
Preparation: 5 minutes
Cooking: 20 minutes

Place egg yolks, cream, and milk in a double boiler and heat to scalding, stirring often. Make a paste of the flour, butter, and mace. Add this to the egg yolk mixture and cook until smooth and creamy, stirring constantly. Add lobster meat and salt. Simmer 12 to 15 minutes and add sherry. Serve on buttered toast points or noodles.

4 egg yolks, slightly beaten
1½ cups heavy cream
1/3 cup milk
2 tablespoons flour
1/3 cup soft butter
⅛ teaspoon mace
2 cups lobster meat
Salt to taste
2 tablespoons sherry or Madeira

"A very rich recipe. Serve with salad and a light dessert."
Beverly Vermilyea

BAKED STUFFED CLAMS

Serves: 4
Preparation: 5 minutes
Cooking: 25-30 minutes

Sauté garlic, onion, parsley, oregano, and bread crumbs in oil for 2 minutes, mixing thoroughly. When onion and garlic begin to brown, remove from heat. Mix with minced clams and juice. Spoon into four large or eight small clam shells. Sprinkle lightly with Parmesan cheese and additional bread crumbs. Bake at 375° for 25 to 30 minutes until crusty.

1 10 ½-ounce can minced clams, undrained
1 teaspoon minced garlic
1 teaspoon diced onion
1 teaspoon chopped parsley
½ teaspoon oregano
¼ cup flavored bread crumbs
2 tablespoons olive oil
Grated Parmesan cheese

Beverley Brainard Fleming

BEER BATTER POLKA

Serves: 8
Preparation: 15 minutes (plus 2 hours refrigeration)
Cooking: 15 minutes
Freeze: Yes

Mix first 6 ingredients and refrigerate 2 hours before using. Beat egg whites until stiff and fold into batter. Coat fish and fry until golden.

1½ cups flour
2 egg yolks
¼ teaspoon pepper
½ teaspoon salt
1 tablespoon corn oil
2/3 cup beer
2 egg whites
2 pounds white fish (flounder, haddock, etc.), cut into bite-sized pieces

Mrs. Henry S. McNeil

FILLET DE SOLE VERONIQUE

Serves: 4
Preparation: 1 hour
Cooking: 30 minutes

SOLE:
Skin and wash fillets; pat dry. Lay in buttered ovenproof dish. Sprinkle lightly with lemon juice and cover with a mixture of white wine and water (approximately half and half, or all wine can be used if desired). Cover with slices of onion, add peppercorns, and bay leaf. Cover with the washed bone of the fish; poach in a slow oven for 20 to 30 minutes. Meanwhile, peel and pit grapes. Put in warm place between two plates to get hot.

SOLE:
1¼ to 1½ pounds fillet of sole
Lemon juice
White wine
1 onion, sliced in rounds
Peppercorns
1 bay leaf
4 ounces white grapes

SAUCE:
Strain off the liquor from the sole and reduce to ¼ cup. Melt 1 tablespoon butter in a saucepan, stir in flour, add milk and stock and reduce to the right consistency. Adjust seasoning and add remaining butter, melted. Place fillets on a hot dish. Pour the sauce over the fillets, arrange grapes at the side, and serve immediately.

SAUCE:
2 tablespoons butter
1 tablespoon flour
1 cup milk
¼ cup very strong fish stock or fumet reduced from liquor

Mrs. Henry S. McNeil

SOLE FILLETS PORT ROYAL

Serves: 4-5
Baking: 1 hour

Combine parsley, eggs, lemon peel, celery seed, half of the chopped pimento, salt, pepper, and cream. Add ¾ of the crab meat and gently blend into the above mixture. Spread fillets flat. Place the mixture on each fillet. Roll fillets up from small end to form a loose roll. Fasten each roll with two wooden picks. Place in a well-greased baking pan. Combine butter, almonds, lemon juice, wine, and the remaining crab meat and pimento. Pour evenly over fillets. Bake in a preheated oven at 325° for 1 hour. Cover for the first 45 minutes and uncover for the last 15 minutes. When ready to serve, remove picks and garnish with parsley, lemon slices, and avocado slices.

2 tablespoons chopped parsley
2 hard-boiled eggs, chopped fine
Grated peel of 1 lemon
1 teaspoon celery seed
1/3 cup canned red pimento, coarsely chopped
¼ teaspoon salt
¼ teaspoon pepper
2 tablespoons cream
8 ounces backfin crab meat, flaked
1½ pounds sole fillets
½ cup melted butter
¼ cup almond halves
4 tablespoons fresh lemon juice
3 tablespoons Madeira wine
4 sprigs parsley
8 lemon slices
2 avocados, sliced

Eleanor Thompson Pease

BAKED STUFFED SEA TROUT

Serves: 4
Preparation: 30 minutes
Baking: 45 minutes

Preheat oven to 425°. Rub outside of trout with salt and sprinkle with lemon juice. Melt 2 tablespoons of butter in skillet; add onions, celery, and mushrooms, cooking about 5 minutes. Mix croutons, celery, onions, and mushrooms with the remainder of the melted butter. If not entirely moist, add a small amount of water. Sprinkle with Parmesan cheese. Fill trout with stuffing and fasten with skewers and string. Wrap in foil and bake in a shallow pan for 30 minutes. Open foil and bake 15 minutes longer. Baste with melted butter during the last 15 minutes.

1 3-4-pound trout, cleaned and boned (white fish, striped bass, or red snapper can be used)
Salt
Lemon juice
½ pound butter
1 medium onion, chopped
2 stalks celery, diced
¼ pound mushrooms, sliced
6½ ounces croutons
Parmesan cheese

Cheryl K. Gibbs

The Court is an indoor area that resembles an urban courtyard or village square of the late eighteenth to early nineteenth century. The Court is paved with Belgian blocks from Wilmington, Delaware, and stone slabs from Harper's Ferry, West Virginia. Framing the Court are four facades: a Connecticut River Valley house (1700-1800), Bannister House (1756), Montmorenci (ca. 1822), and the Red Lion Inn (1800-1825).

Set outside the Red Lion Inn is a brown-painted hexagonal pine and maple table made in Pennsylvania, 1750-75. The Inn served as a local gathering place and also offered lodging for travelers. Men could partake of food and drink and exchange news while relaxing in Windsor chairs such as this sack-back example of hickory and pine, probably made in New England, 1765-95.

Cornish Game Hens with Cranberry Stuffing are served on a large pewter dish made in England, 1700-1740. Pewter was used in taverns because of its durability. When it finally became damaged or worn, the pewter could be melted down and reworked. The smaller pewter plate was made by Stephen Barnes of Middletown or Wallingford, Connecticut, 1791-1800. Mocha ware, an inexpensive utilitarian ware, was also used in taverns. The mocha-ware pitcher and mugs shown here were probably made in Staffordshire, England, 1800-1825, and have engine-turned creamware bodies colored with sgraffito slips. Some mocha ware is decorated further by adding mocha "tea," a liquid tobacco mixture, to the wet surface. The tobacco reacts by spreading into forms resembling trees or the markings on mocha stone — hence the name "mocha ware."

Our setting is completed by a copper and glass lantern with diamond and star piercings, made in the United States, 1825-75; a brown and white linen napkin; a horn and steel knife made by John Ashmore of Philadelphia, 1833-50; a horn and steel fork made in England, 1825-1900; and a red and green plaid wool cloak, probably made in England, 1815-30.

CORNISH GAME HENS WITH CRANBERRY STUFFING

Serves: 2-4
Preparation: 30 minutes
Baking: 1 hour

To prepare stuffing, bring to a boil in a saucepan the chicken broth, cranberries and sugar. Reduce heat and simmer uncovered for 15 minutes, or until berries begin to pop. Meanwhile, sauté celery and onion in butter. Stir stuffing and cranberry mixture into vegetables. Remove giblets from Cornish game hens; wash and pat dry. Season inside and out with pepper and seasoned salt. Stuff lightly with cranberry stuffing. Put any remaining stuffing in ovenproof casserole dish. Tie legs and dot hens with butter. Bake at 350° for 1 hour. After 30 minutes, put dish of stuffing in oven.

2-4 Cornish game hens
½ cup chicken broth
1 cup fresh cranberries
3 tablespoons sugar
½ cup chopped celery
1/3 cup chopped onion
½ cup butter
7 ounces herb stuffing mix
Pepper
Seasoned salt

Elizabeth Tufts Brown

SUPREMES DE VOLAILLE A BLANC

Serves: 4
Preparation: 30 minutes

CHICKEN:
Rub chicken breasts with drops of lemon juice and sprinkle lightly with salt and pepper. In a heavy 10-inch flameproof casserole with cover, heat butter until foaming. Quickly roll breasts in butter. Sprinkle white pepper over them, cover, and place in oven preheated to 400°. After 6 minutes, press tops of breasts with finger. If still soft, return to oven for a few more minutes. They are done when springy and resilient. Do not over cook. Remove chicken from casserole, reserving butter. Place chicken on hot serving dish. Cover and keep warm while making sauce.

CHICKEN:
4 chicken breasts, skinned and boned
½ teaspoon lemon juice
¼ teaspoon salt
Black pepper to taste
4 tablespoons butter
Pinch white pepper

WINE AND CREAM SAUCE:
Pour stock or bouillon and wine into casserole with reserved butter and boil down rapidly over high heat until liquid is syrupy. Pour in cream and boil rapidly until slightly thickened. Season with salt, pepper, and lemon juice. Pour sauce over chicken breasts, sprinkle with parsley, and serve immediately.

WINE AND CREAM SAUCE:
¼ cup white or brown stock or canned beef bouillon
¼ cup port, Madeira or dry white vermouth
1 cup heavy cream
Salt
White pepper
Lemon juice
2 tablespoons fresh minced parsley

Emily Scoville

THE DEVON CHICKEN

Serves: 8
Preparation: 30 minutes (1 day in advance)
Baking: 1 hour
Freeze: Yes

The night before serving, mix sour cream, lemon juice, Worcestershire sauce, celery seed, paprika, garlic, salt, and pepper. Add chicken to this mixture. The day of serving, roll chicken in stuffing mix. Place in greased dish. Pour melted butter over chicken and bake at 350° for 1 hour. Make a sauce combining the mushroom soup, sherry, and parsley. Pour over baked chicken.

8 boned chicken breasts
1 pint sour cream
2 tablespoons lemon juice
2 teaspoons Worcestershire sauce
¼ teaspoon crushed celery seed
1 teaspoon paprika
1 clove garlic, minced
½ teaspoon salt
⅛ teaspoon pepper
1 bag herbed stuffing
½ cup butter, melted
1 10 ½-ounce can golden mushroom soup
¼ cup finely chopped parsley
1-2 tablespoons sherry

"Great dinner to prepare in advance."
   Barbara Morris

LEMON CHICKEN BREASTS

Serves: 4
Preparation: 15 minutes
Baking: 45 minutes

Melt butter in an 8-inch square baking dish. Add clove garlic. Flatten chicken breasts, then fold envelope-fashion and roll in seasoned bread crumbs. Place chicken in baking dish and bake at 350° for 30 minutes, basting occasionally. Add lemon juice and bake for an additional 15 minutes.

Louise Sloane

4 chicken breasts, boned, split, and skinned
¼ cup butter
1 clove garlic, pressed
Seasoned bread crumbs, approximately 1 cup
¼ cup lemon juice, freshly squeezed

CHICKEN BREASTS
A LA BLANC

Serves: 8
Preparation: 30 minutes
Baking: 3 hours

Dust chicken in flour and brown in butter in heavy skillet. Pour on warm sherry. Mix tomato paste and flour together. Mix chicken stock into tomato mixture until smooth. Remove chicken breasts and place in heavy covered baking dish. Pour stock mixture into pan drippings. Simmer until sauce thickens. Slowly stir in sour cream. Season with salt, pepper, jelly, and cheese. Pour sauce over chicken and cover tightly. Bake at 275° for 3 hours. Twenty minutes before chicken is done, sauté mushrooms in butter. Garnish chicken with mushrooms and serve with rice.

4 chicken breasts, split, boned, and skinned
Flour for dusting
6 tablespoons butter
4 tablespoons sherry, warmed
1 tablespoon tomato paste
2 tablespoons flour
1 cup chicken stock
¾ pint sour cream
Salt and pepper
2 tablespoons red currant jelly
4 tablespoons grated Parmesan cheese
2 ½ cups fresh whole mushrooms
3 tablespoons butter

"Very flavorful sauce."
    Mrs. Kathleen Swank

CHICKEN IN
ORANGE SAUCE

Serves: 4
Preparation: 20 minutes
Cooking: 35 minutes

Brown chicken pieces in butter and remove from skillet. To drippings add flour, salt, and spices. Stir into a paste and add orange juice and Tabasco sauce. Cook and stir until thick. Add chicken, almonds, and raisins, simmering 35 minutes or until cooked. Five minutes before serving, add orange sections. Serve with rice.

1 frying chicken, cut up
2 tablespoons flour
¼ teaspoon salt
¼ teaspoon cinnamon
⅛ teaspoon ground cloves
1½ cups orange juice
¼ teaspoon Tabasco sauce
½ cup finely chopped almonds
½ cup raisins
1 orange, sectioned, or 1 can mandarin oranges

Karla Stuck Tobar

Tin-glazed earthenware posset pot, 1660-80

CHICKEN MALO

Serves: 4
Preparation: 30 minutes
Baking: 30 minutes
Freeze: Yes

MAIN DISH:

Quarter ham slices. Pound chicken breasts with meat mallet until ⅛-inch thick. Place two-quarters of each ham slice on one half of the chicken breast. Fold over and seal edges. Repeat process with remaining chicken breasts and ham. Combine bread crumbs, parsley, and pepper. Dip each chicken breast in flour, then beaten egg, then crumb mixture. Melt butter; brown chicken in skillet over medium high heat, about 4 minutes per side. Place in baking dish and bake at 350° for about 20 minutes or until tender.

SAUCE:

Melt butter in a small saucepan. Stir in flour, salt, and pepper. Add milk all at once. Cook and stir over medium heat until thickened and bubbly. Reduce heat to low and add 1 cup of cheese, stirring to melt. Serve at once over chicken.

Cheryl K. Gibbs

MAIN DISH:
2 slices boiled ham
4 chicken breasts, boned and split
2/3 cup fine, dry bread crumbs
1 tablespoon parsley
⅛ teaspoon pepper
¼ cup flour
1 egg, slightly beaten
¼ cup butter

SAUCE:
2 tablespoons butter
2 tablespoons flour
¼ teaspoon salt
Dash pepper
1¼ cups milk
1 cup Swiss, Cheddar, or Gruyère cheese, shredded

CHICKEN MICHELLE

Serves: 4
Preparation: 10 minutes
Cooking: 30 minutes

Mix the spices and flour thoroughly and coat the chicken. Fry in butter until lightly brown. Add onion and fry until onion is soft. Add wine and cook until lightly thickened. Pour into serving dish and keep warm. In the same frying pan, mix instant gravy with water and let thicken. Add heavy and light cream slowly and cook on medium heat until hot. Pour over chicken and serve.

Sylvia Bisbe

1½ pounds boneless chicken breasts, cubed
½ teaspoon salt
⅛ teaspoon paprika
⅛ teaspoon curry powder
¼ teaspoon tarragon
⅛ teaspoon pepper
1 teaspoon flour
1 tablespoon butter
1 large onion, finely chopped
½ cup white wine
1 tablespoon instant brown gravy mix
1/3 cup water
1/3 cup heavy cream
1/3 cup light cream

CHICKEN MARENGO

Serves: 6
Preparation: 30 minutes
Baking: 50 minutes

Coat chicken with flour seasoned with salt, pepper, and tarragon. Reserve any remaining flour. In a frying pan, quickly brown chicken on all sides in the oil and butter. Place chicken in a heavy casserole or Dutch oven. Add the reserved flour to the remaining oil and butter in the frying pan and gradually whisk in the wine. After the sauce is thick and smooth, add to the chicken. Then add the tomatoes, garlic, and mushrooms. Bake in covered casserole at 350° for about 50 minutes or until the chicken is tender.

Catherine H. Maxwell

6-8 boneless chicken breasts
½ cup flour
1 teaspoon salt
½ teaspoon pepper
1 teaspoon tarragon
¼ cup oil
¼ cup butter
1 cup dry white wine
2 cups canned tomatoes with liquid
1 clove garlic, minced
¼ pound mushrooms, sliced

CHICKEN ASPARAGUS CASSEROLE

Serves: 6
Preparation: 1 hour
Baking: 15-20 minutes

Melt 6 tablespoons of butter in skillet and brown chicken quickly until cooked throughout; drain. Melt 4 tablespoons butter in saucepan and sauté shallots. Blend in flour; add salt and pepper. Stir in cream and white wine gradually. Add half of cheese and stir until it melts. Arrange asparagus in buttered shallow baking dish. Put chicken breasts on top and pour sauce over all. Sprinkle with remaining cheese. Bake at 375° for 20 to 25 minutes.

"Can be prepared ahead of time and refrigerated."
  Margaret Coveney

10 tablespoons butter
4 whole chicken breasts, skinned, boned, and quartered
6 shallots, finely chopped
4 tablespoons flour
1 teaspoon salt
½ teaspoon pepper
1½ cups light cream
½ cup dry white wine
½ cup freshly grated Parmesan cheese
24-32 asparagus spears, cooked until barely tender and drained

CHICKEN TETRAZZINI

Serves: 8-10
Preparation: 3 hours

Quarter chickens, cover with boiling water and simmer until tender, approximately 25 minutes. Add 1 tablespoon salt to water after chicken begins simmering. Let chickens cool in broth, then remove and cut meat into fine strips. Add skin and bones to broth and simmer until only 2 cups of broth remain. Strain. This may take up to 2 hours.

Slice mushrooms very thin and sauté in 3 tablespoons of butter until soft and slightly browned. In a large frying pan melt 3 tablespoons of butter and blend with flour. Gradually stir in the chicken stock and stir until sauce is smooth and thickened. Add heavy cream, sherry, pepper, salt and nutmeg to taste and cool for 10 minutes, stirring constantly.

Cook spaghetti in salted boiling water about 5 minutes or until just tender. Drain. Place in large buttered casserole. Mix chicken, mushrooms, and sauce together and pour over spaghetti. Sprinkle with Parmesan cheese and brown lightly in a moderate oven. If increasing recipe, turkey makes a good substitute.

Mrs. John Learned

2 3-pound chickens
1 pound fresh mushrooms
1 pound very thin spaghetti
6 tablespoons butter
2 tablespoons flour
1 cup heavy cream
3 tablespoons sherry
Salt and pepper
Nutmeg
¾ cup Parmesan cheese

TURKEY TATERS

Serves: 8
Preparation: 30 minutes
Baking: 25 minutes

Cut potatoes in half horizontally. Scoop out, leaving thin shell. Set skins aside. In a large bowl, cut potatoes into small pieces. Add celery, onion, mayonnaise, sour cream, garlic salt, pepper, and mustard. Mix thoroughly. Stir in turkey. Fill each potato skin approximately half full. Bake 12 to 15 minutes at 400°. Slice cheese and place one slice on each potato. Return to oven and bake 8 to 10 minutes or until cheese is melted.

Patricia Campbell

4 large potatoes, baked
½ cup chopped celery
½ cup chopped red onion
1 cup mayonnaise
1 cup sour cream
1½ teaspoons garlic salt
¼ teaspoon pepper
1 tablespoon prepared mustard
2 cups cubed, cooked turkey
Cheddar cheese

CHICKEN DIVAN

Serves: 8
Baking: 30 minutes

Place cooked broccoli in a 9 x 13-inch buttered casserole; cover with chicken. Make a sauce of chicken soup, mayonnaise, evaporated milk, cheese, and curry powder. Mix and spread over casserole. Sprinkle with slivered almonds and bread crumbs. Bake at 350° for about 30 minutes.

Ellen Dannaway

2 bunches broccoli, cooked and drained
4 cups cooked chicken, chopped
1 10½-ounce can cream of chicken soup
2/3 cup mayonnaise
½ cup evaporated milk
½ cup Cheddar cheese, grated
½ teaspoon curry powder
Slivered almonds
Bread crumbs

CHICKEN FROMAGE

Serves: 6
Preparation: 30 minutes
Baking: 45 minutes
Freeze: Yes

Add garlic to melted butter and let stand 20 minutes. Mix together bread crumbs and cheese. Salt and pepper chicken cutlets and dip in melted margarine, then crumb mixture. Place in 9 x 13-inch baking dish. Pour remainder of melted margarine over chicken. Bake uncovered at 350° for 45 minutes. Baste occasionally with pan juices, if desired.

Norma Adams

6 cutlets or 3 whole chicken breasts, skinned and split
1 clove garlic, minced
½ cup melted butter
1 cup fine dry bread crumbs
½ cup finely grated sharp Cheddar cheese
¼ cup grated Parmesan cheese
Salt and pepper

SASSY CHICKEN

Serves: 4
Preparation: 30 minutes
Cooking: 20 minutes

Sauté onion and mushrooms in butter until tender. Sauté breasts sprinkled with salt and pepper until done. Remove breasts and add vermouth to pan, bringing to boil quickly. Blend in sour cream; add parsley to taste. Place breasts on rice and pour mixture over all. Garnish with parsley.

Bobbi Bruni

1 large onion, chopped
6 large fresh mushrooms, chopped
¼ pound butter
4 chicken breasts, boned
Salt and pepper to taste
½ cup dry vermouth
2 cups sour cream
Parsley to taste
4 servings rice, cooked

CHICKEN DIJON

Serves: 4-6
Baking: 1 hour

Melt butter and combine with oil. Set aside half of the mixture. To the other half add mustard, chives, basil, and peppers. Combine with wire whisk or food processor until mixture is the consistency of heavy cream. Salt chicken lightly, brush with butter and oil mixture that has mustard added, making sure all sides are well covered. Roll in bread crumbs. Line 9 x 13-inch baking pan with foil. Add part of the remaining butter and oil mixture, coating the bottom of the pan well. Place chicken breasts in baking pan and bake at 375° for approximately 1 hour. Baste as necessary with remaining oil and butter mixture. If crumbs begin browning too quickly, cover pan lightly with tent of foil.

8 chicken breasts, skinned and boned
½ cup butter
½ cup oil
6 tablespoons Dijon-style mustard
6 tablespoons fresh chopped chives
½ teaspoon dried basil
Dash black pepper
Dash cayenne pepper
Salt
2 cups fine bread crumbs

"This makes an excellent picnic entree, as it is good cold as well as hot."
Barbara C. Heiken

CHICKEN IN RASPBERRY CREAM SAUCE

Serves: 8
Preparation: 45 minutes
Cooking: 45 minutes

Dredge chicken in flour and sauté chicken in butter and oil; remove from pan and set aside. Add raspberry vinegar to pan and bring to boil. Remove from heat and add chicken and chicken stock. Simmer 10 to 15 minutes. Remove chicken, set aside, and keep warm. Boil liquid over high heat until it has thickened to the consistency of cream. Add whipping cream and allow to thicken over medium heat. Serve over chicken.

3 tablespoons butter
8 chicken breasts, skinned and boned
2 tablespoons oil
¾ cup raspberry vinegar
1¼ cup chicken stock
1¼ cup whipping cream

"This is delicious served with rice pilaf, a green salad, and French bread."
Diane Hamilton Sanders

Brass teakettle, 1710-40

The first Chinese porcelain came to Europe as ballast on ships carrying spices and silks. Europeans found porcelain beautiful and very different from the stoneware and earthenware they produced. Porcelain became a major export to Europe in the seventeenth century, and by 1785 the United States had entered the China trade.

At first, Europeans were satisfied with native Chinese wares. But by the early eighteenth century, they were sending prints and European designs to be copied on porcelain by Chinese artists. Conversely, European factories began imitating Chinese forms and designs. The pebbly "orange peel" surface — not found on European work — is prized by collectors because it indicates a genuine piece of Chinese export porcelain.

This group of Chinese export porcelain made between 1785 and 1810 is only a small selection of the pieces from a large service: a pierced fruit basket and tray, salt, covered tureen containing Green Beans Estill and platter with Crown Roast of Pork. Also shown are three horn and steel knives made in England or the United States, 1820-50.

VEAL
A L'ORANGE

Serves: 4-5
Preparation: 30 minutes
Baking: 30 minutes

VEAL:
Pound veal cutlets until very thin. Season with salt and pepper. In a skillet, sauté the veal in butter over high heat turning them several times until lightly browned. Do not let the butter burn. Arrange the veal in a shallow baking dish and cover the dish with a lid or sheet of aluminum foil. Bake at 300° for about 20 minutes.

SAUCE:
Add shallots to the veal juices in the skillet and sauté them until they are soft and transparent. Stir in the lemon and orange juices, the orange-flavored liqueur, and the lemon and orange rinds. Simmer the mixture over low heat, stirring to remove all the brown bits from the bottom of the pan. Stir the milk into the flour and add the mixture to pan. Cook the sauce, stirring over low heat until it is smooth and thick (at first it may appear to curdle, but this will disappear as it thickens). Add chicken stock and mushrooms. Remove from heat and stir in sour cream. Season sauce with salt and pepper and pour over veal just before serving.

"Always receives rave comments. Serve on rice."
Joan B. Gallagher

VEAL:
6 veal cutlets, each ¼-inch thick
Salt and pepper to taste
¼ cup butter

SAUCE:
2 tablespoons finely chopped shallots
Juice of 1 lemon
Juice of 1 orange
¼ cup orange-flavored liqueur
2 teaspoons grated orange rind
2 teaspoons grated lemon rind
1 cup milk
2 tablespoons flour
1 cup chicken stock
½ pound mushrooms, sliced
¼ cup sour cream
Salt and pepper to taste

VEAL CHOPS
IN CASSEROLE

Serves: 6
Preparation: 30 minutes
Baking: 45 minutes

Sauté onions until translucent in a skillet large enough to hold the chops; remove from pan and reserve. Put ½ cup of clarified butter in skillet. When butter is hot, place well-seasoned veal chops in it. When browned on both sides, remove the cooking fat, add white wine and beef stock, then add the bouquet garni and the garlic cloves. Let simmer for a few minutes, then add the onions and mushrooms. Place all in an ovenproof casserole dish. Bake covered at 350° for about 45 minutes or until the meat is tender.

Winterthur Archives 𝓜

½ cup clarified butter
12 veal chops, 1-inch thick
Salt and pepper
1 cup white wine
1 cup beef stock
Bouquet garni of 2 sprigs parsley, 2 stalks celery, 1 bay leaf, 1 sprig thyme
6 garlic cloves, crushed
6 onions, sliced and fried
2 pounds mushrooms, sliced

VEAL VEZELAY

Serves: 8-10
Preparation: 4 hours (1 day in advance)
Baking: Approximately 3 hours

VEAL STOCK:

For best results, make the stock a day in advance. Put veal bones and veal cubes in a large kettle. Cover with cold water. Add salt and peppercorns. Bring the mixture slowly to a boil. Skim fat from surface and add onions stuck with cloves. Add parsley, celery, carrot, and thyme. Cover the kettle and simmer the stock slowly for 3 hours. Strain the stock through a fine sieve lined with cheesecloth and let it cool, uncovered. Chill the stock and remove the layer of fat before using. Makes about 4½ cups.

VEAL VEZELAY:

Place a 6-pound veal roast on rack in roasting pan. Roast at 350° for about 2½ hours or until meat is tender and done, basting frequently with 2 cups veal stock. If a meat thermometer is used, it should register 175°. Cool the veal, reserving the pan juices, and cut the meat into thin slices. Melt butter, blend in flour, and gradually add 2½ cups veal stock and Parmesan cheese. Cook the sauce, stirring until it is thick and smooth. Spread the veal slices with half of the sauce and press the slices together to reshape the meat roast. Cover the meat with the remaining sauce and sprinkle the top and sides with fine dried bread crumbs. Arrange the meat on an ovenproof platter or in a shallow casserole. Heat the reserved pan juices and deglaze the pan with Madeira or cream sherry. Pour the juices around the meat and bake at 450° for about 10 minutes or until the crumbs are nicely browned.

VEAL STOCK:

3½ pounds veal bones
1 pound veal, cut into cubes
3 quarts cold water
1 tablespoon salt
12 peppercorns
2 large white onions, each stuck with 1 clove
2 sprigs parsley
1 stalk celery, with leaves
1 carrot, quartered
½ teaspoon thyme (or a sprig of fresh thyme)

VEAL VEZELAY:

6-pound veal roast
4½ cups veal stock
4 tablespoons butter
2 tablespoons flour
1 cup freshly grated Parmesan cheese
Bread crumbs
¼ cup Madeira or cream sherry

"A change from the usual chicken, beef, or pork. An elegant entree."
Anne Y. Wolfe

Iron fork and turner, 1835

GOOD ENOUGH FOR COMPANY BEEF BURGUNDY

Serves: 4-6
Preparation: 30 minutes
Baking: 3 hours
Freeze: Yes

Combine all ingredients in casserole or Dutch oven (no need to brown beef). Cover and bake at 325° for 3 hours. Serve with noodles or rice. To extend, add 1 pound more beef, ¼ cup wine and 1 tablespoon tapioca.

2 pounds stew beef or chuck steak, cubed
1 10 ½-ounce can onion soup
1 10 ½-ounce can cream of mushroom soup
½ cup ketchup
2-3 tablespoons tapioca
½ cup burgundy wine
½ pound fresh mushrooms, sliced

"A fool-proof recipe."
Marian Evans

LASAGNA

Serves: 4-6
Preparation: 15 minutes
Cooking: 40 minutes

MEAT FILLING:
In large skillet brown the meats; drain off fat. Add rest of meat filling ingredients and simmer uncovered for 5 minutes. Meat mixture can be prepared ahead and refrigerated.

MEAT FILLING:
½ pound ground sausage
½ pound ground round steak
½ cup chopped onions
½-1 clove garlic, minced
3 tablespoons fresh chopped parsley
1½ teaspoons fresh basil
1½ teaspoons fresh oregano
½ teaspoon salt
¼ teaspoon pepper
6 ounces tomato paste

CHEESE FILLING:
Prepare cheese filling by combining cottage cheese or ricotta cheese, egg, and Parmesan cheese. According to package directions, cook lasagna noodles to make 2 layers in pan. In a 9 x 13-inch pan, make two layers each of noodles, meat filling, and cheese filling. Top with mozzarella slices and brush with milk. Bake at 375° for 20 to 25 minutes.

CHEESE FILLING:
1 cup creamed cottage or ricotta cheese
1 egg
¼ cup grated Parmesan cheese
Lasagna noodles
Mozzarella cheese
Milk

Karol A. Schmiegel

BEEF STROGANOFF I

Serves: 4
Preparation: 1 hour
Cooking: 25 minutes

Pour ½ cup of boiling water over the dried mushrooms and soak for 1 hour. Reserve liquid and chop mushrooms. Trim all fat from meat and cut into large, bite-sized pieces. Melt butter in skillet and brown meat. When cooked to desired doneness, remove to heated platter. Add the brandy to butter and juices in skillet and heat for 1 minute, swirling around pan. Add more butter as needed, cooking the fresh mushrooms slowly for approximately 3 minutes. Add onion, garlic, and dried mushrooms, and cook until onions soften, approximately 3 minutes. Remove from heat and add flour, mushroom powder, mustard, beef stock, and mushroom liquid. Stir, turning on heat again, until flour is well blended. Return the meat to skillet; mix in and heat thoroughly. Reduce heat to low or warm. Add sour cream and dill. Stir until cream is melted and blended. Do not let boil. Serve with steamed rice seasoned with lemon pepper.

Karol A. Schmiegel

6 dark dried European mushrooms
1½ pounds fillet of beef
4 tablespoons butter
½ cup Armagnac, other brandy, or dry sherry
¼ pound fresh mushrooms, sliced
½ cup finely chopped onions
2 cloves garlic, minced
2 tablespoons flour
¼ teaspoon mushroom powder
1½ tablespoons Moutarde de Meaux (Pommeray)
½ cup beef stock
1 cup sour cream (or less, to taste)
1/3 cup chopped dill
Rice
Lemon pepper

BEEF CUBES IN WINE SAUCE

Serves: 6
Preparation: 25 minutes
Baking: 4-5 hours

Brown beef cubes quickly in oil. Place in casserole or Dutch oven and season with salt and pepper. Pour heated brandy over beef and ignite. Brown mushrooms in butter and add them to the meat. In the same butter, add tomato paste, Kitchen Bouquet, and flour. Mix until smooth. Add this mixture and remaining ingredients to meat, combining well. Bake at 275° for 4 to 5 hours.

Joyce McClung

3 pounds lean beef, cubed
1-2 tablespoons oil
Salt and pepper to taste
3 tablespoons Grand Marnier or brandy (if using brandy, add ½ orange peel grated very fine)
2 cups fresh mushroom caps
2 teaspoons tomato paste
2 teaspoons Kitchen Bouquet
4 tablespoons flour
2 10 ½-ounce cans consommé
12 small white onions
½ cup red wine

BEEF STROGANOFF II

Serves: 8
Cooking: 4 hours

Wash beef and pat dry. Lightly sprinkle with garlic powder and onion salt. Broil beef until rare (do not overcook). Let cool. Cut beef into 1½-inch cubes and set aside. In a large Dutch oven combine soups, water, dill weed, celery leaves and garlic powder; heat until boiling, stirring occasionally. Add onions and mushrooms. Bring mixture to a light boil. Add beef and wine. Bring mixture to a light boil again, stirring frequently. Reduce heat until mixture simmers, stirring constantly. Cook uncovered for 4 hours, stirring mixture every 15 to 20 minutes. Stir in sour cream just before serving. Heat through. Serve stroganoff over noodles.

John H. Meszaros

3-4 pounds of lean London broil
Garlic powder
Onion salt
2 10½-ounce cans cream of mushroom soup
2 10 ½-ounce cans golden mushroom soup
¼ cup water
1 tablespoon dill weed
1½ tablespoons dried celery leaves
¼ teaspoon garlic powder
2 large onions, diced
1 cup sliced mushrooms (or 1 6-ounce can sliced mushrooms, drained)
¼ cup red Bordeaux or cabernet sauvignon wine
1 pint sour cream
Wide egg noodles

Iron cauldron, 1700-1800

HEARTY BEEF STEW

Serves: 8
Preparation: 30 minutes
Baking: 5-6 hours
Freeze: Yes

Trim any extra fat from meat and place in 4-quart casserole (browning beef is not necessary). Add all other ingredients in the order given and stir well. Bake at 250°, covered, for 5 to 6 hours. Stir about once each hour and remove cover for last hour of cooking. If the dish is to be frozen, potatoes should not be added until ready to reheat.

Neva B. Murphy

3 pounds lean stew beef
1 28-ounce can whole tomatoes, broken slightly with spoon
½ can beef bouillon
½ cup white wine
1 pound small white onions
20 ounces peas and carrots combined (frozen may be used)
2 pounds small whole potatoes
4 tablespoons tapioca
½ cup fine bread crumbs
1 bay leaf
½ teaspoon seasoned salt
¼ teaspoon pepper

SIRLOIN TIPS IN RED WINE

Serves: 8
Preparation: 45 minutes
Baking: 2-3 hours

Combine flour, paprika, salt, and pepper in brown paper bag. Shake well. Add beef and shake until each cube is well coated. Brown meat in butter, using heavy aluminum or iron pan. Meat must be well browned. Transfer meat from pan to a heavy casserole. Empty all excess fat, but do not scrape pan. Return pan to heat. Add consommé, garlic, and flavor enhancer. Bring to a boil and scrape pan thoroughly. Immediately pour over meat in casserole. Add 1 cup of wine in covered casserole. Bake at 300° until tender, approximately 2 to 3 hours. As liquid evaporates, add remaining wine.

Mrs. W. Ellis Preston

4 pounds sirloin tips or round of beef, cut in 1-inch cubes
1 cup flour
6 teaspoons paprika
2 teaspoons salt
1 teaspoon pepper
¼ pound butter
1 10½-ounce can beef consommé
1 small garlic, finely diced
2 teaspoons flavor enhancer
1½ cups dry red wine

BOEUF BOURBON

Serves: 6
Preparation: 30 minutes
Baking: 3 hours

Place olive oil and garlic in Dutch oven. Add meat and brown on all sides. Add 1 cup bourbon, water or stock, lemon juice, lemon rind, salt, paprika, pepper, bay leaves, and cloves. Cover and bake at 325° for 2½ hours. Uncover and baste meat with pan juices. Return to oven for ½ hour or until nicely browned. Cooking time is for well done roast. Cooking time may be reduced for rarer beef. Remove beef to heated serving platter; keep meat warm. Remove lemon rind and bay leaves from pan juices. Mix cornstarch with 2 tablespoons bourbon. Slowly add to hot pan juices stirring constantly. Simmer for 2 minutes. Pour some sauce over meat and pass the remainder in a sauce boat.

4 pounds beef, bottom round or rump, in 1 piece
4 tablespoons olive oil
2 cloves garlic, finely chopped
1 cup plus 2 tablespoons bourbon
1 cup water or stock
Juice of ½ lemon
Rind of ½ lemon, cut in 8 pieces
1 teaspoon salt
1 teaspoon paprika
½ teaspoon freshly ground black pepper
2 bay leaves
3 cloves
1 tablespoon cornstarch

John Krill

LONDON BROIL STUFFED WITH MUSHROOMS AND CHEESE

Serves: 4
Preparation: 5 minutes (plus time to marinate, if desired)
Cooking: 10-12 minutes

Have butcher cut lengthwise pocket in steak. Marinate if desired. Sauté mushrooms in 1 tablespoon of butter for 2 minutes. Combine mushrooms, cheese, remaining 1 tablespoon butter, garlic, ½ teaspoon of salt, and ⅛ teaspoon of pepper. Stuff pocket with mushroom mixture. Fasten with skewers or toothpicks. Sprinkle steak with remaining salt and pepper. Refrigerate until shortly before serving time. Broil about 3 inches from heat for 5 to 6 minutes on each side depending on size and thickness of steak. Place on warmed platter. Slice in thin diagonal slices against the grain.

1 3-pound London broil
2 tablespoons butter
½ pound fresh mushrooms, sliced (or 2 4-ounce cans sliced mushrooms, drained)
2 tablespoons crumbled blue, Roquefort, or Cheddar cheese
1 clove garlic, crushed
1 teaspoon salt
¼ teaspoon pepper

"Quick, elegant way to serve London broil. Serve with potatoes, fresh green beans, and salad."
Beverley Brainard Fleming

ADONNA'S GREEK MEATBALLS

Serves: 15-20 for cocktail buffet; 6-8 for entree
Preparation: 30 minutes
Cooking: 30-40 minutes
Freeze: Yes

Combine chili sauce, jelly, and lemon juice in large saucepan and heat slowly to boil. Make meatballs of desired size from first four ingredients and drop gently into boiling sauce. Simmer for 30 to 40 minutes. Meatballs will absorb more of the sauce if they are made a day ahead and reheated just before serving. If ground beef is not entirely fat-free, chill after cooking and remove fat from top before reheating.

Marian Blakeman

- 2 pounds very lean ground beef
- 1 large egg, slightly beaten
- 1 onion, finely chopped
- 1 teaspoon salt
- 1 12-ounce bottle chili sauce
- 1 10-ounce jar grape jelly
- 1 tablespoon lemon juice

EGGPLANT CASSEROLE

Serves: 4
Preparation: 30 minutes
Baking: 2 hours (1 day in advance)

Prepare one day before serving to allow flavors to intermingle. Slice and peel eggplant about ½-inch thick and place in bowl of salted water for a few minutes. Drain, rinse, and dry eggplant. Beat eggs with water, salt, and pepper in a shallow dish. Dip eggplant in egg batter and then in bread crumbs. Brown in bacon fat and olive oil and set aside. Brown ground beef until no pink is left and set aside. Butter large casserole and layer as follows: 1) eggplant slices; 2) onion, parsley, pepper, and oregano; 3) ground beef; 4) tomatoes and juice. Add salt and pepper and sprinkle with Italian herbs. Repeat layers until ingredients are gone. Pour any remaining egg batter over this. Top with leftover bread crumbs, adding additional bread crumbs if desired. Sprinkle with cheese and top with bacon strips. Bake uncovered at 350° for 2 hours. Reheat on day of serving.

Nancy Richards

- 1 large eggplant
- 2 eggs
- 1 tablespoon water
- Salt and pepper
- Seasoned bread crumbs
- Olive oil
- 8 strips bacon
- 1 pound ground chuck
- 2 medium onions, sliced
- ½ cup chopped fresh parsley
- 2 medium green peppers, sliced
- 1 tablespoon oregano
- 1 large can tomatoes
- 1 teaspoon mixed Italian herbs
- Parmesan cheese

BARBEQUE BRISKET

Serves: 8-10
Preparation: 20 minutes
Cooking: 3-4 hours
Freeze: Yes

Remove all fat from brisket. Place brisket in a heavy skillet and brown on both sides. Add onions and garlic and brown. Add remaining ingredients. Cover and simmer 3 to 4 hours until very tender.

6-pound beef brisket
2 large onions, sliced
1 clove garlic, minced
¾ cup brown sugar
½ cup vinegar
1 cup ketchup
½ tablespoon salt

"Best if prepared the day before serving."
   Virginia S. Baldwin

MOUSSAKA

Serves: 6-8
Preparation: 45 minutes
Baking: 45 minutes

MOUSSAKA:
Sauté onions and meat in 6 tablespoons butter. Add diluted tomato paste, parsley, salt, and pepper. Simmer for 45 minutes. In the meantime, peel eggplants, slice ¼-inch thick, fry in oil, and drain. Rub baking dish with remaining butter. Spread most of bread crumbs on bottom of pan; reserve small amount for topping. Alternate layers of eggplant and meat mixture, sprinkling grated cheese between each layer. Reserve some cheese for topping. Top layer should be meat.

MOUSSAKA:
3 onions, finely chopped
2 pounds lean chopped lamb or beef
¼ pound butter
1 cup tomato paste, diluted with ½ cup water
2 tablespoons chopped fresh parsley
Salt and pepper
3 eggplants
1 cup oil
½ cup bread crumbs
1 cup grated Parmesan or Romano cheese

MOUSSAKA TOPPING:
Beat eggs well. Add milk, flour, and butter. Spread over top layer of meat. Sprinkle remaining grated cheese over top. Sprinkle with remaining bread crumbs. Bake at 350° for 45 minutes.

MOUSSAKA TOPPING:
4 eggs
1 quart milk
4 tablespoons flour
¼ pound butter

Mrs. John Learned

LAMB STEW WITH VEGETABLES

Serves: 20
Cooking: 2 hours

Cut the meat in large pieces, season with salt and pepper, and brown in the hot butter. When meat is well browned on all sides, remove the fat and reserve. Add the flour, blending it well with the meat. Cook in a hot oven for 5 minutes. Add the stock or water, bouquet garni, garlic, tomatoes, salt, and pepper. Mix well with a wooden spoon and bring to a boil, stirring continuously. Meanwhile, brown the onions and turnips in the same fat. Add a pinch of sugar and add to the stew. Add the potatoes, correct the seasoning and let simmer until cooked, about 30 minutes. Add the peas, carrots, and string beans to the stew and cook for 15 minutes. Before serving, remove the bouquet, the garlic, and the fat that appears on the surface. Serve very hot with fresh chopped parsley.

Winterthur Archives

6 pounds lean lamb or mutton from shoulder parts of ribs or breast
Salt and pepper to taste
2 tablespoons butter
2 tablespoons flour
Enough stock or water to cover 2/3 of meat
1 bouquet made of 4 sprigs parsley, 2 branches celery, 1 bay leaf, and 1 sprig thyme
4 cloves garlic, crushed
2 fresh tomatoes, coarsely chopped
24 small onions
6 turnips, cut lengthwise and in pieces
Pinch of sugar
1 pint shelled peas
6 carrots, cut lengthwise and in pieces
1 pint green beans, cut up
18 small potatoes
1 tablespoon chopped parsley

Brass shaker, 1775-1825

STUFFED CROWN ROAST OF PORK

Serves: 10-12
Preparation: 15 minutes
Baking: 2½ hours

Preheat oven to 350°. Cover exposed bones on roast with foil to prevent burning during cooking; set aside. In large skillet, cook apple, celery, and onion in butter until tender but not browned. Add chicken broth, cinnamon, salt, cloves, and pepper. Cover; simmer over low heat 5 minutes. In large bowl combine bread crumbs, parsley, dried fruit, and egg. Pour vegetable mixture over bread mixture, mixing lightly. Lightly fill center of roast with some of the stuffing. Place roast on rack in baking pan. Bake 2½ hours or approximately 35 minutes per pound. After 1 hour, cover stuffing in center of roast to prevent burning. Spoon remaining stuffing into baking dish. Bake stuffing during last hour of roasting pork.

4½-5-pound crown roast of pork (about 12 ribs)
1 cup chopped, peeled apple
1 cup chopped celery
½ cup chopped onion
¼ cup butter
¾ cup chicken broth
¼ teaspoon ground cinnamon
⅛ teaspoon salt
Dash ground cloves
Dash pepper
4 cups fresh ½-inch bread cubes
¼ cup chopped parsley
1 8-ounce package dried apricots or peaches, cut up
1 egg, slightly beaten

Elizabeth J. Barlow

LAMB CREOLE

Serves: 6
Preparation: 30 minutes
Cooking: 1½ hours

Sauté bacon lightly and reserve fat. Saute the lamb in very hot oil and bacon fat combined. Stir lamb to brown evenly on all sides. Do not let pieces touch. Remove meat, then add onions, bacon, and garlic. Cook slowly for 5 minutes. Add the flour and brown. Remove from heat. Stir in tomato purée, wine, and 1¼ cups stock. Blend until smooth. Return to heat, bring to a boil, and then add meat, herbs, and seasonings. Cover and simmer 1 to 1½ hours on top of the stove or in oven at 350°, stirring occasionally. Add reserved stock if needed.

2 pounds leg of lamb, cut into 1-inch squares
2 tablespoons peanut or olive oil
2 medium onions, sliced
6 slices bacon, cut in 1-inch pieces
1 clove garlic, chopped
2 tablespoons flour
1 teaspoon tomato purée
½ cup white wine
1¾ cups lamb or chicken stock
Salt and pepper
Bouquet of herbs (parsley, bay leaf, and basil)

"Very good with fresh garden vegetables and spring lamb. Goes well with Creole Rice."
  Margaret Norton

PORK CHOPS PENNINGTON

Serves: 6-8
Preparation: 5 minutes
    (marinate overnight)
Cooking: 30-35 minutes

Combine first eight ingredients in a shallow baking dish and mix well. Add meat to marinade. Cover and marinate overnight in refrigerator. Remove chops from marinade, and place about 4 to 5 inches from the coals on a grill. Grill over slow to medium coals from 30 to 34 minutes or until no longer pink, turning and basting occasionally.

½ cup vegetable oil
¼ olive oil
¼ cup lemon juice
3 cloves garlic, crushed
1 tablespoon salt
1 teaspoon paprika
½ teaspoon pepper
6 bay leaves, halved
6-8 (1-inch thick) loin or rib pork chops

Ellis Coleman

PORK CHOPS DIJONNAISE

Serves: 4
Cooking: 1 hour

Salt chops and dredge in flour. Brown in heavy skillet in small amount of fat; remove from pan. In the same skillet, sauté onion until soft and translucent. Remove from pan and add to pork. Saute mushrooms in pan; return pork and onions. Add vermouth; cover and simmer until tender, approximately 30 to 40 minutes. Remove chops; to pan juices, add mustard, capers, and chicken stock. Mix egg yolk and heavy cream slightly and add a small amount of pan juices to warm. Slowly add egg yolk mixture to pan stirring constantly until smooth and thickened. Pour over chops just before serving.

4 pork chops
½ teaspoon salt
¼ cup flour
1 large onion, thinly sliced
¼ pound mushrooms, sliced
¼ cup dry vermouth
1 teaspoon Dijon mustard
1 teaspoon chopped capers
¼ cup chicken stock
1 egg yolk
¼ cup heavy cream

Peggy Frankenburg

PORK CHOPS RUSKIN

Serves: 4
Preparation: 30 minutes
Cooking: 10-15 minutes

Cut meat into strips 2-inches long by ½-inch wide. Sauté in butter just until meat is cooked through. Stir in sour cream and heat to boiling point, but do not boil. Stir in curry powder, salt and pepper to taste. Serve over green noodles or rice.

8 pork chops, trimmed
3 tablespoons butter
2 cups sour cream
1-3 teaspoons curry powder
Salt and pepper

Joyce Longworth

SAUSAGE CASEROLE

Serves: 10
Preparation: 30 minutes
Baking: 1 hour

In a large skillet, brown sausage, onion, and pepper, crumbling sausage as it browns. Add uncooked rice. Transfer to a casserole dish and add soup mix, boiling water, celery, and black olives, if desired. Bake uncovered at 350° for 45 minutes. Add almonds and bake another 15 minutes.

2 pounds mild pork sausage
1 medium onion, chopped very fine
1 medium green pepper, chopped very fine
1 cup uncooked rice
2 packages dry chicken noodle soup mix
5 cups boiling water
1½ cups diced celery
Black olives, sliced (optional)
½ cup slivered almonds

"Serve with green vegetable and fruit salad. Makes a wonderful brunch dish and may be prepared ahead of time."
  Grace Barrington

OXTAIL RAGOUT

Serves: 6-8
Preparation: 1 hour
Cooking: 3-3½ hours (one day in advance)
Freeze: Yes

The day before serving, brown oxtails in butter in large skillet. Remove to larger casserole. Add to casserole the peppers, celery, onions, garlic, parsley, Worcestershire sauce, salt and pepper, chicken and beef stocks, and red wine. Simmer for 3 to 3½ hours until meat is tender when pierced with fork. Remove meat from casserole. Strain juices. Put meat in one container and juices in another container, leaving both in the refrigerator overnight. The next day, remove the layer of fat at the top of the juice container. Return meat and juice to the casserole. Sauté mushrooms in sweet butter for 5 minutes until slightly browned. Boil carrots and onions in chicken stock and water until tender. Decoratively arrange mushrooms, carrots, and onions on oxtails in casserole. Bake at 350° until hot and bubbly.

8 pounds oxtails
3 tablespoons butter
2 green peppers, sliced
4 stalks celery, cut into 2-inch pieces
2 onions, sliced
1 clove garlic, crushed
1 cup parsley
1 tablespoon Worcestershire sauce
Salt and pepper
4 cups chicken stock
4 cups beef stock
½ cup dry red wine
1 pound mushrooms, quartered if large
2 tablespoons sweet butter
6 medium carrots, cut into 2-inch lengths
1 pound pearl onions
1 cup chicken stock
1 cup water

Eli Bauman

CALVES' LIVER WITH HERBS

Serves: 12

LIVER:

Moisten liver slices with milk, dredge them with flour, and place in a saucepan with hot clarified butter. Cook over moderately hot flame. When browned on one side, turn over, and cook a few more minutes until browned. Season with salt and pepper. Liver should not be cooked too much, as it becomes tough. When cooked, arrange the slices on a hot serving dish and pour the sauce over them. Garnish with crisp bacon and watercress.

SAUCE:

Toss the sweet butter in the pan until soft. Add parsley, tarragon, and lemon juice and mix well together. Correct the seasoning and pour the sauce over the liver. Serve very hot.

Winterthur Archives 𝓜

LIVER:

1 slice calves' liver per person, ¼-inch thick
1 cup milk
½ cup flour
½ cup clarified butter
Salt and pepper to taste
Bacon
Watercress

SAUCE:

½ cup sweet butter
1 teaspoon chopped parsley
1 teaspoon chopped tarragon
Juice of 1 lemon

PAT'S BOURBON SAUCE FOR STEAK

Yield: 8 jars
Preparation: 30 minutes

Chop chutney finely. Mix all ingredients well and bottle.

17 ounces Major Grey's Chutney
1 14-ounce bottle ketchup
1 12-ounce bottle chili sauce
1 10-ounce bottle A-1 sauce
1 10-ounce bottle Worcestershire sauce
½ cup bourbon, or more to taste

Geraldine T. Nesbitt

Tin-glazed earthenware food warmer, ca. 1750.

Accompaniments

Accompaniments include a variety of foods from vegetables to pasta. This kitchen setting displays an assortment of foods in many types of containers: new potatoes in a copper pan with a brass bail, made in England or the United States, 1775-1820; onions and macaroni in cylindrical glass jars with domed covers and deep blue bands, made in the United States, 1840-75; hot peppers in a burl bowl made in America, 1700-1800; pea pods in a spatterware bowl made in England, 1810-40; vegetables in a brass colander made in England or America, 1725-1800; mushrooms and turnips on a breadboard probably made in the United States, 1800-1900, The table was made in America, ca. 1800. The steel and oak chopper was made in America, 1750-1850; the copper measuring spoon was made in England or America, 1700-1800; the fabric of the blue, brown, and white plaid linen curtains was woven in the United States, 1800-1875.

Precautions were taken to protect collection objects that came in contact with food during the photography for this cookbook. Objects selected for use were first reviewed by the conservators. Ceramic objects were examined for stability, with particular attention to cracks and chips in the glaze, since damage might result from the absorption of liquid by the porous ceramic material. Metal objects were lacquered before use to prevent food from coming into direct contact with the metal surface. In some cases, reproductions or objects from Winterthur's study collection were substituted for less stable pieces.

All foods were prepared without salt, which might corrode delicate surfaces. Immediately after photography was completed, the foods were removed from the objects, which were then wiped clean, rinsed with warm water, and dried with a soft cloth. After reexamination by conservators, museum objects were returned to exhibition areas.

CAULIFLOWER POLONAISE

Serves: 6
Cooking: 30 minutes

Clean cauliflower of all stems. Wash and parboil, then cook in hot salted water to which has been added 1 tablespoon of milk per quart of water. Cook cauliflower until tender, about 20 to 25 minutes. When cooked, place in a colander to dry, then arrange each flower in a vegetable dish. Season with salt and pepper. Sprinkle the chopped egg over the top. Meanwhile, melt the sweet butter in a large frying pan. Add the bread crumbs and stir constantly over the heat until the bread crumbs become golden. Pour immediately over the cauliflower. Sprinkle a little fresh chopped parsley over the top and serve.

1 head cauliflower
Salt and pepper
½ hard-boiled egg, chopped
½ cup sweet butter
½ cup fresh bread crumbs
Fresh parsley, chopped

Winterthur Archives

SPINACH AND ARTICHOKE CASSEROLE

Serves: 6
Preparation: 15 minutes
Baking: 25 minutes

Cook frozen vegetables. Place artichoke hearts in bottom of a buttered 2½-quart casserole. Combine cream cheese, butter, and lemon juice. Add spinach to cheese mixture and put in casserole. Put croutons on top and cover. Bake at 350° for 25 minutes.

2 packages frozen chopped
   spinach
1 package frozen artichoke
   hearts or 2 14-ounce cans
   artichoke hearts
8 ounces cream cheese,
   softened
¼ pound butter, softened
2 tablespoons lemon juice
Buttered croutons

Fay Gates

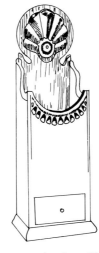

Mahogany pipe box, 1760-75

SAVORY SPINACH

Serves: 6
Preparation: 20 minutes
Baking: 30 minutes

Blend cream cheese and spinach together. Add remaining ingredients and spoon mixture into small casserole. Bake at 350° for about 30 minutes.

1 package frozen chopped spinach, cooked and drained
3 ounces cream cheese, softened
½ cup sour cream
3 strips bacon, cooked and crumbled
¼ cup chopped green onion
1 tablespoon horseradish

BAKED SPINACH

Serves: 6
Preparation: 20 minutes
Baking: 20-25 minutes

Cook and drain spinach; mix with other ingredients. Pour the mixture into a 10 x 6 x 1½-inch baking dish. Bake at 350° for 20 to 25 minutes or until set.

10-ounces spinach, chopped
3 eggs, slightly beaten
2 tablespoons soft butter
1 teaspoon Worcestershire sauce
3 teaspoons chopped onion
1 cup sharp Cheddar cheese, shredded
1/3 cup milk
1 teaspoon salt
½ teaspoon thyme
1 cup rice, cooked

Mrs. Rosemary Moores

Painted tulip spoon rack, 1750-1800

RUNNERS' RATATOUILLE

Serves: 4-6
Cooking: 20 minutes

Sauté garlic in oil, then remove. Add onions, carrots, celery, and eggplant. Reduce heat and cook 3 minutes. Add spices, zucchini, yellow squash, and diluted tomato paste. Cook over low heat until vegetables are thoroughly coated. Add tomatoes. Cook on low heat for 1 minute. Turn mixture into oiled casserole. Sprinkle with grated cheese. Broil in oven until cheese melts. This can also be made in an electric skillet.

2-3 tablespoons olive, sunflower, or peanut oil
3-4 cloves garlic
1 small onion, thinly sliced
2 carrots, sliced
2 stalks celery, sliced
1 small eggplant, thinly sliced
Fresh basil, oregano, parsley, salt and pepper, as desired
1 medium zucchini, sliced
1 medium yellow squash, sliced
1 6-ounce can tomato paste diluted with ½ cup water
2 garden-ripe tomatoes, quartered (or small can of tomatoes)
1 cup grated Romano or Parmesan cheese

"Other vegetables can be substituted depending upon availability. For a crunchy taste, add cup of raw sunflower seeds."
   Janice Roosevelt

RATATOUILLE AND SAUSAGE

Serves: 6
Preparation: 1 hour

In heavy 6-quart pan, heat oil to medium temperature and cook onion and garlic for 2 to 3 minutes. Add eggplant and cook for another 5 minutes. Add peppers and cook 5 minutes. Add zucchini, tomatoes, and seasonings; cover pan and simmer for 15 minutes. If vegetables are too dry, add some tomato liquid. Simmer sausages for approximately 10 minutes in enough boiling water to cover them; drain well and add to simmering vegetables. Continue cooking, covered, for 30 minutes, stirring occasionally. Serve large portions for main course or smaller portions as an accompaniment.

½ cup oil
2 large onions, sliced
3 cloves garlic, minced
1 medium eggplant, cut into 1-inch cubes
2 green peppers, chopped
3 zucchini, cut into ½-inch slices
1 2-pound can whole Italian tomatoes, drained (reserve liquid)
1 teaspoon salt
1 teaspoon sugar
1 teaspoon oregano
½ teaspoon thyme
¼ teaspoon pepper
12 sweet Italian sausage links

Catherine H. Maxwell

SOUR CREAM GREEN BEAN CASSEROLE

Serves: 10-12
Preparation: 30 minutes
Baking: 40 minutes
Freeze: Yes

Cook beans until tender. Mix the butter, cornstarch, salt, pepper, sugar and onions and cook until thick. Toss with beans, add sour cream and bacon or mushrooms, if desired, and place in a 2-quart baking dish. Combine several crackers and cheese in a blender, making crumbs. Top casserole with cracker and cheese mixture. Dot with butter and bake 40 minutes at 375°.

2 large bags frozen French-style green beans or 4 9-ounce packages
4 tablespoons butter
2 tablespoons cornstarch
1 teaspoon salt
½ teaspoon pepper
2 teaspoons sugar
1 teaspoon onion salt (or freshly diced onion)
1 cup sour cream
Crackers
2 slices of Swiss cheese
Four slices bacon, cooked and crumbled (optional)
½ pound mushrooms, sautéed lightly in butter (optional)

"This is a different type of green bean casserole, nice for a buffet. May be prepared a day in advance."
Patti Bullen

GREEN BEANS ESTILL

Serves: 6
Cooking: 20 minutes

Simmer beans in a minimum of water until cooked to desired tenderness. In a separate pan, fry bacon until crisp and remove from pan. Cook onion in 3 tablespoons of bacon fat until dark brown. Add flour to onion. Stir in bouillon and simmer until smooth. Pour over hot drained beans and toss. Crumble bacon over top.

2 pounds fresh green beans
8 slices bacon
1 medium onion, thinly sliced
1 tablespoon flour
½ cup beef bouillon

Wylma P. Davis

FRENCH PEAS

Serves: 4
Cooking: 20 minutes

Wash and remove hearts from lettuce, leaving hollow cores. Shell peas and place in hollow cores of lettuce. Sprinkle with salt and pepper, and add a pinch of sugar and some butter. Wrap each head in cheese cloth; tie top. Place lettuce in pan with tight fitting lid. Add 1/3 cup boiling water. Replace lid, turn down heat, and simmer 20 to 30 minutes. Remove wrapped heads from pot. Place on individual serving dishes, then carefully remove cheese cloth. Dot with butter and sprinkle with chopped parsley. Serve both lettuce and peas.

Variation: Cook 2 dozen tiny white onions or 1 cup of fresh scallions. Add to peas before serving.

4 small heads Boston or Bibb lettuce
1-1½ pounds fresh peas
Salt
Pepper
Pinch of sugar
Butter
Parsley, chopped

"This is a great way to use fresh garden peas and lettuce. Use butter and lemon juice if on a low sodium diet."
Margaret Norton

ZUCCHINI CASSEROLE

Serves: 10-12
Preparation: 15 minutes
Baking: 25 minutes

In large saucepan, cook zucchini in boiling salted water until tender, about 5 minutes. Drain. In medium skillet, cook bacon until crisp; remove from pan. Add onion and garlic to the skillet and sauté until the onion is tender. Drain. Stir onion-bacon mixture into drained zucchini. Add remaining ingredients except Parmesan cheese and toss until well coated. Spoon zucchini into a 13 x 9 x 2-inch baking dish. Sprinkle with Parmesan cheese. Bake at 350° for 20 minutes or until bubbly.

Cheryl K. Gibbs

7-8 medium zucchini, cut into ¼-inch slices
1 cup water
8 slices bacon, diced
1 large onion, chopped (about 1 cup)
1 large clove garlic, minced
4 slices white bread, diced
2 cups shredded Cheddar cheese
1 teaspoon salt
1 teaspoon Italian seasoning
Dash pepper
1 15-ounce can tomato sauce
¼ cup grated Parmesan cheese

Stoneware jug, 1725-50

ZUCCHINI AND CORN AU GRATIN

Serves: 6-8
Preparation: 20 minutes
Baking: 25-35 minutes

Trim off ends of zucchini. Split lengthwise into halves, then into quarters. Cut each quarter into ½-inch pieces. Place zucchini in steamer over boiling water. Cover and steam approximately 5 minutes or until firm but not mushy. Shuck corn. Place no more than 6 ears at a time in unsalted boiling water; cook 3 minutes, remove at once and drop into iced water. Drain. Cut the corn kernels from cob. There should be approximately 2¼ cups. Melt 2 tablespoons of butter in heavy saucepan. Add flour, stirring with a wire whisk. When blended, add cream slowly, stirring rapidly with whisk until thickened and smooth. Add nutmeg and cayenne, cooking a few minutes while stirring constantly. Add Cheddar cheese and stir. Turn off heat and add salt and pepper to taste. Fold drained zucchini and corn into cream sauce. Pour mixture into a shallow baking dish and sprinkle with Parmesan cheese. Dot with remaining 1 tablespoon of butter. Bake at 350° for 25 to 30 minutes or until golden brown and bubbly. If desired, broil briefly to get a better glaze on top.

Carol K. Baker

1½ pounds zucchini
7-8 ears corn
3 tablespoons butter
3 tablespoons flour
2 cups light cream
⅛ teaspoon grated nutmeg
1/16 teaspoon cayenne pepper
3 tablespoons grated sharp Cheddar or Gruyère cheese
Salt and freshly ground pepper
¼ cup grated Parmesan cheese

TIPSY ZUCCHINI SAUTE

Cooking: 8 minutes

Sauté onion gently in butter for 2 minutes. Add zucchini and stir gently for 5 minutes over low heat. Do not over cook or let get mushy. Add wine and simmer about 1 minute. Add almonds and serve hot. As an alternative, substitute apple juice and sunflower seeds for wine and almonds.

Kathryn K. McKenney

1 onion, chopped
2 tablespoons butter
3 cups sliced young zucchini
¼ cup white wine (or ¼ cup apple juice)
¼ cup slivered almonds (or 2 tablespoons sunflower seeds)

CHEESY ZUCCHINI

Serves: 4-6
Preparation: 20 minutes
Baking: 30 minutes

Sauté onions in oil for 5 minutes. Do not brown. Add sliced zucchini, cooking and stirring for 10 minutes or until slightly softened. Turn off heat. Add sour cream to which nutmeg has been added. Layer zucchini mixture and cheese in a 2-quart casserole, ending with the zucchini. Sprinkle a heavy layer of crumbs across top to completely seal. Add a sprinkling of Parmesan cheese if desired. Bake at 350° for 30 minutes.

Kathryn K. McKenney

2 large onions, sliced
Oil
3 small zucchini, sliced (5 cups)
1½ cups sour cream
⅛ to ¼ teaspoon nutmeg
½ pound mild cheese, such as mozzarella or Monterey Jack
Toasted bread crumbs
Parmesan cheese (optional)

POTATO KUGEL

Serves: 4-6
Preparation: 30 minutes (with food processor)
Baking: 1 hour

Preheat oven to 375°. Peel potatoes, cut in eighths, and place in a large bowl filled with cold water. Peel onion. Process to fine consistency. Drain juice and place onion in medium bowl. Pour oil to depth of ¼-inch in a 13 x 9 x 2-inch pan; place in oven to heat. Process potatoes to fine consistency. Drain liquid by pressing in strainer. Work as quickly as possible to avoid discoloration. Combine all ingredients except oil. Spoon into pan, working carefully to avoid splashing hot oil. Return to oven and bake 1 hour or until top is brown. Cut into squares to serve.

Dena N. Forster

6 large potatoes
1 onion, grated
Vegetable oil (approximately ½ cup)
3 eggs
½ cup flour
½ teaspoon baking powder
1½ teaspoons salt
⅛ teaspoon pepper

PARTY POTATOES

Serves: 8-10
Preparation: 45 minutes
Baking: 1 hour

Blend the cream cheese and sour cream in small bowl and set aside. Mash potatoes thoroughly until smooth. Add cream cheese mixture and beat well. Stir in chives. Add salt and pepper to taste. Spread in 9 x 13-inch buttered pan. At this point potatoes may be covered and put in refrigerator. One hour before serving dot with butter, and sprinkle with cheddar cheese and paprika. Bake at 325° for 1 hour.

Anna V. Harford

8-10 potatoes, peeled and cooked
8 ounces cream cheese, softened
8 ounces sour cream
3 tablespoons chives
Salt and pepper to taste
Garlic salt (optional)
Butter
1 cup grated Cheddar cheese
Paprika

CAPONATA ST. MIHIEL

Serves: 6
Cooking: 45 minutes

Sauté onion in olive oil about 5 minutes but do not brown. Add cubed eggplant and cook about 10 minutes, stirring to distribute heat evenly. Add pine nuts, sesame seeds, and pepper. Taste and add more pepper if desired. While cooking, if it is necessary to add more liquid, more vinegar or white wine may be added. Add celery, tomatoes, vinegar, and capers. Simmer gently over low heat for 30 minutes, stirring occasionally.

2 medium onions, chopped
½ cup olive oil
2 eggplants, unpeeled, chopped into ½ inch cubes
½ cup pine nuts
½ cup toasted sesame seeds
Freshly ground black pepper
White wine (if desired)
1 cup diced celery
2½ cups fresh or canned tomatoes
¼ cup red wine vinegar
2 ounces capers (or to taste)

"Can be served as a hot vegetable dish, used as a cold salad, or served hot or cold on sandwiches. Especially good put into a pita pocket with cheese and heated."
  Kathryn K. McKenney

SCALLOPED EGGPLANT

Serves: 8 as accompaniment or 4 as entree
Preparation: 20 minutes
Baking: 30 minutes

Place onions in bowl and set aside. Peel eggplant and dice in ¾ inch pieces. Put in saucepan with salt and cold water to cover. Bring to boil and simmer until tender but not mushy. Drain thoroughly. Beat eggs until well blended. Add cottage cheese, thyme, and nutmeg. Blend thoroughly and let sit for 5 minutes. Add and stir in grated cheese and salt. Combine gently with eggplant cubes and onions. Turn mixture into buttered 2-quart baking dish (9 x 9 x 2-inch). Be sure onions and eggplant are distributed equally. In saucepan, melt butter in hot water. Toss well with stuffing mix. Spoon evenly over eggplant mixture. Bake uncovered at 350° for 30 minutes until set and browned. Let casserole sit 5 to 10 minutes before serving. Cut into squares. This can be made ahead and refrigerated until half an hour before baking.

1 cup frozen small whole onions
1 medium eggplant, 1½ to 2 pounds
1 teaspoon salt
3 eggs, well beaten
1 cup large curd cottage cheese
⅛ teaspoon dried thyme
Dash grated nutmeg
1 cup grated Cheddar cheese
½ teaspoon salt
4 tablespoons butter
1/3 cup hot water
2 cups herb-seasoned stuffing mix

"This dish is a very satisfying entree. I serve it with a cold tomato and broccoli salad with a vinaigrette dressing."
  Joyce Ford Halbrook

BAKED EGGPLANT WITH GARLIC

Preparation: 5 minutes
Baking: 40 minutes

Wash eggplant and cut off top. Cut lengthwise in slices ½-inch thick. Rub cut surfaces with oil, and sprinkle with salt and pepper. Mix garlic and parsley and distribute on surface of each slice of eggplant. Arrange in layers in baking dish. Pour over remaining oil, cover with foil, and bake at 350° for 40 minutes. May be served hot or cold.

Dena N. Forster

1 large eggplant
½ cup olive oil
Salt and pepper to taste
4 cloves garlic, crushed
3 tablespoons parsley, minced

SICILIAN SURPRISE

Serves: 8
Preparation: 20 minutes
Cooking: 40 minutes

Combine first 4 ingredients with oil and cook 10 minutes. Add remaining ingredients and simmer 20 to 30 minutes, or until vegetables are tender. Serve as a side dish or over pasta.

3 cups eggplant, chopped
½ cup green pepper, chopped
1 onion, chopped
2 cloves garlic, chopped
½ cup olive oil
1 cup tomato paste
4 ounces mushrooms, sliced
¼ cup water
½ cup stuffed olives, sliced
1½ teaspoons sugar
½ teaspoon oregano
Salt and pepper
Worcestershire sauce

VANNIE'S TOMATO CASSEROLE

Preparation: 10 minutes
Baking: 1 hour

Brown tomatoes and onions in butter, adding sugars. Let cook for 10 minutes until a little thick. Add the bread cubes and stir. Bake at 300° for 1 hour. If bubbling too much, reduce temperature to 275°.

Ann Layton Scott

2 16-ounce cans tomatoes, drained
2-3 onions, sliced
Butter
¼ cup sugar
¼ cup brown sugar
2-3 slices toasted bread, cubed

RICE CANADIEN

Serves: 6-8
Preparation: 10 minutes
Cooking: 1 hour

Heat rice, onions, celery, and butter in a large saucepan over medium heat, stirring frequently for 5 minutes. Add remaining ingredients. Simmer covered for about 1 hour, stirring frequently.

1 cup brown rice, uncooked
1 cup wild rice, uncooked
1 cup chopped onions
1 cup sliced celery
¼ pound butter
1 pound fresh mushrooms, sliced
1 quart chicken broth
½ cup snipped fresh parsley
½ teaspoon salt
¼ teaspoon thyme
¼ teaspoon pepper

SOUTHERN RICE

Serves: 6-8
Preparation: 35 minutes
Baking: 20 minutes
Freeze: Yes

Cook rice according to directions and season with nutmeg. Place half of rice in a well-greased 2-quart casserole. Layer half of soup, almonds, and mushrooms on top of rice. Layer remaining rice, soup, and mushrooms; top with almonds. Melt butter and pour over entire casserole. Bake at 350° for 20 minutes or until well heated. If freezing, melted butter should not be added until ready to heat.

1 cup rice
½ teaspoon nutmeg
1 can cream of mushroom soup
1 6-ounce can mushrooms, drained
2½ ounces slivered almonds
½ cup butter

"Excellent with baked ham or roast and a green salad or vegetable."
   Neva B. Murphy

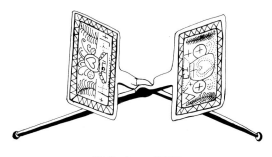

Wafer iron, 1757

CREOLE RICE

Serves: 6
Preparation: 20 minutes

Cover cooked rice with a cloth and place over a bowl of warm water or in 325° oven to keep warm. Trim mushrooms and cut in thick slices. Skin tomatoes, removing seeds and juice. Cut tomatoes into quarters or eighths, depending on size. Cut peppers into fine slices and parboil one minute. Drain and blanch in cold water. Sauté mushrooms, peppers, and rice. Season and toss gently with a fork. Do not overcook. Serve with Lamb Creole.

2 cups rice, cooked
½ pound fresh mushrooms
2 fresh tomatoes
2 green peppers
2 tablespoons butter
Salt

Margaret Norton

BARLEY PILAF

Serves: 4
Preparation: 15 minutes
Baking: 1 hour
Freeze: Yes

In an ungreased 5-cup casserole, mix all ingredients except parsley. Cover and bake at 325° until done, about 1 hour. Stir in parsley.

2 tablespoons butter
2/3 cup uncooked barley
2 tablespoons minced onion
2 teaspoons chicken bouillon
½ teaspoon celery salt
¼ teaspoon pepper
2 cups boiling water
2 tablespoons snipped fresh parsley

"Marvelous with poultry or veal."
   Jo Smith

SWEET POTATO SOUFFLE WITH SHERRY AND WALNUTS

Serves: 6
Preparation: 30 minutes
Baking: 30 minutes
Freeze: Yes

Whip all ingredients except walnuts until light. Place in a 1½-quart casserole and bake at 350° until golden, about 30 minutes. Sprinkle walnuts over top.

1 quart mashed sweet potatoes
½ cup sherry
¼ teaspoon salt
½ cup brown sugar
2 eggs, beaten
½ cup butter
½ cup black walnuts, chopped

Norma Adams

TOMATOES FLORENTINE

Serves: 6
Baking: 10 minutes

Cook spinach until just tender. Strain or pat dry. Melt butter in pan. Sauté scallions briefly until tender. Add spinach, cream, nutmeg, salt, pepper and stir. Remove from heat. Cut stem end out of tomatoes. Slice tomatoes in half and score the inside lightly to spread the tomato in half slightly. Mound 1/6 of the spinach mixture on each half and place in flat baking dish. Sprinkle spinach mounds with cheese. Bake at 350° for 10 minutes. Place under broiler for 1 minute just before serving.

"The tomato and spinach flavors complement one another beautifully."
   Kate Wheeler

1 pound fresh or frozen spinach, chopped
1 tablespoon butter
1 tablespoon finely chopped scallions (optional)
¼ cup heavy cream
¼ teaspoon freshly ground nutmeg
¼ teaspoon salt
Dash pepper
3 large tomatoes
Parmesan or Romano cheese

SQUASH CASSEROLE

Serves: 4
Preparation: 15 minutes
Baking: 30 minutes

Cut squash in large pieces and cook gently in water until tender. Drain. Add other ingredients and mix well. Place in a buttered casserole and cover with bread crumbs. Bake at 350° for 20 to 30 minutes.

Mrs. A. Keith Pooser

1½ pounds squash
½ pound sharp Cheddar cheese, grated
½ cup mayonnaise
½ cup slivered almonds
1 egg, beaten
½ teaspoon salt
¼ teaspoon pepper
Bread crumbs, parsley, paprika

SESAME CARROTS

Serves: 6
Preparation: 10 minutes
Cooking: 10 minutes

Sauté onions in margarine over medium heat until soft. Add carrots. Sprinkle sesame seed, ginger, salt and pepper over all. Stir occasionally, cooking approximately 5 minutes or until done. Recipe can also be prepared as a stir-fry dish using higher heat.

Mary Ann Roder

2 tablespoons margarine
1 medium-sized onion, chopped
4 cups thinly sliced carrots
4 tablespoons whole sesame seed
½ teaspoon ground ginger
Salt and pepper to taste

COUNTRY STYLE GRANOLA

Yield: 5 quarts
Preparation: 30 minutes
Baking: 20 minutes

Melt first six ingredients in large roasting pan. When mixed, let cool slightly, and add dry ingredients, except raisins. Stir thoroughly. Bake in two large pans at 350° for 20 minutes. Stir every 5 to 6 minutes. After granola has cooled, add raisins. Recipe may be doubled, but if ingredients are bought in bulk the cost is about two-thirds that of commercial natural cereals.

½ cup oil (or less)
½ cup butter
2 tablespoons dark molasses
1 tablespoon vanilla
1 cup brown sugar
1 cup honey
2 pounds rolled oats
½ cup sesame seeds
1 cup nuts, chopped
2 cups grape nuts
1 cup wheat germ
1 pound shredded coconut
1 cup sunflower seeds
1 cup raisins

"There is almost as much joy in mixing up granola as in making bread, and, since you never make it exactly the same, it's always an adventure. A jarful tied with a ribbon makes a pleasant gift."
    Nancy M. Patterson

BROCCOLI ONION DELUXE

Serves: 6
Baking: 30 minutes

Slit fresh broccoli spears lengthwise. Cut into 1-inch pieces. Cook in boiling salted water until tender; drain. Cook onions in boiling salt water until tender; drain. In saucepan, melt 2 tablespoons of butter, blend in flour, salt, and pepper. Cook 1 to 2 minutes. Add milk, cook and stir with a whisk until thick and bubbly. Reduce heat and blend in cream cheese until smooth. Place cooked vegetables in a greased 1½-quart casserole. Pour sauce over and mix lightly. Melt remaining butter and toss with crumbs. Sprinkle Cheddar cheese and crumbs on casserole. Bake covered at 350° for 20 minutes, then remove cover and bake 10 minutes more.

Jackie Kelly

1 pound fresh broccoli
2 cups frozen whole small onions or 3 medium onions, quartered
4 tablespoons butter
2 tablespoons flour
¼ teaspoon salt
Dash of pepper
1 cup milk, heated
3 ounces cream cheese
1 cup soft bread crumbs
2 ounces sharp Cheddar cheese, coarsely shredded (½ cup)

CORN PUDDING

Serves: 6
Preparation: 15 minutes
Baking: 1 hour

Mix all ingredients in a 1½-quart baking dish. Place baking dish in shallow pan of water and bake at 350° for 1 hour.

1 box frozen corn, thawed
1 cup milk
½ cup soft bread crumbs
2 eggs, beaten
1 cup shredded Cheddar cheese
1 teaspoon dry mustard
1 teaspoon salt
1 tablespoon onion, chopped
1 tablespoon green pepper, chopped

"A favorite of vegetarians."
  Dora May Shotzberger

SPICY ASPARAGUS

Preparation: 5 minutes
Cooking: 10 minutes

Combine all ingredients and boil gently, being careful not to overcook.

2 cups water
½ cup olive oil
½ cup wine vinegar
1 teaspoon crushed coriander seeds (or ½ to 1 teaspoon ground coriander)
1 teaspoon thyme
½ bay leaf
2 cloves garlic, crushed
Fresh asparagus

"Can be served hot or cold. Good with any variety vegetable, but best with asparagus or artichokes."
  Kathryn K. McKenney

Chinese export porcelain sweetmeat dish, 1740-60

Successful baking has always relied on fresh ingredients, careful measuring, and advice passed from one generation to the next. Today's basic baking tools differ little from those of the eighteenth century. Shown here are copper and brass measuring cups made in Albany, New York, 1835-36; tin-glazed earthenware canisters made in England, 1710-50; and a cherry and burl wood rolling pin made in the Shaker community of New Lebanon, New York, 1800-1900. The smell of homemade sweets, the warmth of the oven, and the homey implements contribute to the comforting atmosphere of a kitchen baking day.

Georgia Peach Pie with braided-edge crust rests on an eighteenth-century breadboard made in the United States. It is surrounded by a brass spice dredger made in England or America, 1750-1800; a glass bowl with plate made in England, 1750-75; ivory and glass hourglass, possibly made in England, 1725-1800; and steel sugar nippers, made in America, ca. 1750. The working surface is a black walnut table made in Pennsylvania, 1675-1710.

OLD-FASHIONED LEMON PIE

Serves: 18
Preparation: 15 minutes
Baking: 25 minutes

Cream butter and sugar; beat in egg yolks. Add water and cornmeal. Add lemon and grated rind. Fold in stiffly beaten egg whites. Pour into pie pans and bake at 350° until brown.

½ cup butter
2 cups sugar
6 eggs, separated
½ cup cold water
2 tablespoons cornmeal
Juice of 2 lemons
Rind of 1 lemon, grated
2 9-inch pie pans lined with
    unbaked crust

Mrs. Adail Christmas

GEORGIA PEACH PIE

Serves: 6-8
Preparation: 2 hours (plus
    1 hour refrigeration
    for crust)
Baking: 1 hour and 15 minutes

PIE CRUST:
Mix dry ingredients and cut shortening into them. Add enough cold water to hold mixture together. Pastry is best if chilled before rolling. Roll out pastry and place in an 11-inch pie plate, leaving enough dough around sides to form a decorative edge. Form edge, prick bottom with a fork, and chill 1 hour. Line shell with wax paper, fill with beans to weight shell, and bake at 425° for 15 minutes. Remove beans and paper, baking 10 minutes longer. Brush with one beaten egg white, and bake 5 minutes or until golden. Allow to cool.

PIE CRUST:
2 cups flour
¾ teaspoon salt
2/3 cup shortening
1/3 cup cold water

FILLING:
Combine sugar, flour, cinnamon, and butter, cutting butter into lumps as you mix. Blanch peaches in boiling water for 2 minutes and plunge immediately into ice water. Peel, stone and slice peaches. Arrange half the slices in concentric overlapping circles and sprinkle with half of the butter-sugar mixture. Add another layer of peaches and top with butter-sugar mixture. Squeeze lemon juice over all. Bake at 375° for 40 minutes or until bubbly. Cool before serving.

FILLING:
2/3 cup brown sugar
2 tablespoons flour
1 teaspoon cinnamon
¼ cup butter
4 pounds peaches
Juice of ½ lemon

MOTHER'S PUMPKIN CUSTARD PIE

Serves: 6-7
Preparation: 10 minutes
Cooking: 35-40 minutes

Warm pumpkin. Add butter and stir until melted. Mix together the flour, sugar, and nutmeg. Stir into warm pumpkin. Beat eggs and add milk. Stir thoroughly into pumpkin mixture and pour into 9-inch unbaked pie shell. Sprinkle top generously with nutmeg. Bake at 450° for 10 minutes. Reduce heat to 375° and bake 25 to 30 minutes longer or until filling is firm.

2 cups fresh pumpkin, mashed
1½ tablespoons butter
2 tablespoons flour
½ cup sugar
½ teaspoon nutmeg
2 eggs
1 cup milk

Mrs. Henry T. Skinner

OPEN SESAME PIE

Serves: 6
Preparation: 35 minutes (plus refrigeration)

Beat milk, egg yolks, ¼ cup of sugar, and salt in top of double boiler until well blended. Cook over hot water until mixture coats spoon. Add the softened gelatin; stir until dissolved. Refrigerate one hour or until almost set, stirring occasionally. Whip cream and fold in mixture. Add vanilla and dates. Beat 2 egg whites, adding 2 tablespoons sugar slowly. Continue beating until stiff. Fold into date mixture. Put into baked pie shell and sprinkle sesame seeds over top. Refrigerate until firm.

1 baked 9-inch pie crust
2-4 tablespoons sesame seeds, toasted (toast at 325° for 8-10 minutes until light golden brown)
1 cup milk
2 eggs, separated
¼ cup sugar
¼ teaspoon salt
1 envelope gelatin, softened in ¼ cup cold water
¾ cup whipping cream
1 teaspoon vanilla
1 cup pitted dates, cut fine
2 tablespoons sugar

Carol K. Baker

Brass monteith, 1700-1730

BLUEBERRY CHIFFON PIE

Serves: 6-8
Preparation: 45 minutes (plus at least 6 hours refrigeration)

Put gelatin and water into a heat-proof glass cup. After gelatin has softened, place the cup in a little boiling water to dissolve gelatin. Set gelatin aside to cool. Wash and drain blueberries; blot with paper towel. Beat eggs until frothy. Add sugar and vanilla and beat again. Add salt.

Stir cooled gelatin into egg mixture. Whip cream and fold it into egg mixture. Put in refrigerator until it begins to set, then carefully fold in blueberries with spoon. Spoon mixture into baked pastry shell. Refrigerate. Cover carefully with foil. Do not touch top of pie with foil.

1 tablespoon unflavored gelatin
¼ cup cold water
1½ cups fresh blueberries
4 eggs
2/3 cup granulated sugar
1 teaspoon vanilla
¼ teaspoon salt
1 cup whipping cream
1 9-inch pastry shell, baked or 1 graham cracker crust

"The delicate gelatin egg-cream mixture enhances the visual appeal and the taste of the blueberries. Best if served the same day it is made".
   Lydia T. Thomen

TAVERN RUM PIE

Serves: 16
Preparation: 1 hour (1 day before serving)
Baking: 10 minutes (crust)

COOKIE CRUMB CRUST:
Crush vanilla wafers into fine crumbs. Combine crumbs with melted butter. Press mixture into bottom and sides of 10-inch pie plate. Bake at 375° about 10 minutes. Cool.

COOKIE CRUMB CRUST:
50 2-inch vanilla wafers (2 2/3 cups)
½ cup melted butter

FILLING:
Beat egg yolks at medium speed until light; gradually add sugar. In saucepan, sprinkle gelatin in water. Bring to boil. Slowly pour into egg mixture, beating at low speed. Whip cream until stiff. Fold into egg mixture, then gently fold in rum. Refrigerate until mixture can be mounded in peaks when dropped from spoon. Heap in crumb crust and refrigerate. At serving time, cut pie into wedges and serve each with a bunch of green grapes.

FILLING:
6 egg yolks
1 cup granulated sugar
1 envelope plus 1 teaspoon unflavored gelatin
½ cup cold water
1 pint heavy cream
½ cup rum

Alberta Melloy

CAROLINA CHESS PIE

Serves: 8
Preparation: 10 minutes
Baking: 50-55 minutes

Mix brown sugar, flour, and butter. Add beaten egg yolks with milk and vanilla. Pour into pastry shell. Bake at 450° for 15 minutes. Reduce heat to 350° and continue baking for 40 minutes or until knife comes out clean. Serve with whipped cream.

Variation:
Add 1 cup of chopped pecans to the pie before baking and garnish with 8 to 10 pecan halves after baking to make pecan pie.

Carolyn M. Lynch

1½ cups brown sugar
1 tablespoon flour
½ cup melted butter
4 egg yolks, well beaten
1 cup milk
1 teaspoon vanilla
1 9-inch unbaked pastry shell

SOUR CREAM PECAN PIE

Serves: 6-8
Preparation: 10 minutes
Baking: 45 minutes

Combine first 6 ingredients in mixing bowl; beat until smooth and well blended. Stir in pecans and pour into chilled pie crust. Bake at 400° for 45 minutes or until knife blade inserted near center comes out clean.

Marian Blakeman

3 eggs
½ cup sour cream
½ cup dark corn syrup
1 cup granulated sugar
1 teaspoon vanilla extract
⅛ teaspoon salt
1 cup whole pecans
1 unbaked 9-inch pie crust

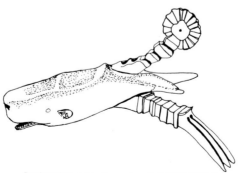

Scrimshaw pastry wheel, 1825-1920

SUGAR AND SPICE PECANS

Yield: 1 pound nuts
Preparation: 10 minutes
Baking: 45 minutes

Beat egg white and water until frothy. Combine salt, cinnamon, and sugar. Add to egg white; stir well. Add pecans and stir until nuts are well coated. Spread on ungreased baking sheet. Bake at 200° for 45 minutes, stirring every 15 minutes. Nuts should be dry and toasty. Store in an airtight container. Keeps well.

Patricia Campbell

1 small egg white
1 tablespoon water
¾ teaspoon salt
1½ teaspoons cinnamon
1 cup sugar
1 pound pecan halves (walnuts may be substituted)

MELT-IN-THE-MOUTH COOKIES

Yield: 6 dozen
Preparation: 1 hour
Baking: 5 minutes per pan
Freeze: Yes

Cream butter. Add sugar, vanilla, and egg. Beat until light. Add sifted dry ingredients and nuts. Drop by scant teaspoonfuls on greased cookie sheet two inches apart. Bake at 375° for 5 minutes. Cool on cookie sheets 2 minutes. Remove to wire rack. Store in refrigerator.

Madalin W. James

½ cup butter
1 cup light brown sugar, packed
1 teaspoon vanilla
1 egg
¾ cup sifted flour
1 teaspoon baking powder
½ teaspoon salt
½ cup finely chopped nuts

CHINESE ALMOND COOKIES

Yield: 3-4 dozen
Preparation: 20 minutes
Baking: 15-18 minutes

Sift together flour, sugar, soda, and salt. Cut sifted mixture into butter until mixture resembles cornmeal. Add egg and almond extract. Mix well. Shape into 1-inch balls and place on cookie sheet. Place an almond on each cookie and press down slightly. Bake at 350° for 15 to 18 minutes. Cool on rack.

Deborah L. Shone

2¾ cups sifted flour
1 cup sugar
½ teaspoon baking soda
½ teaspoon salt
1 cup butter
1 egg, slightly beaten
1 teaspoon almond extract
1/3 cup whole almonds

HUNGARIAN POPPY SEED NUT SLICES

Yield: 6-8 dozen cookies
Preparation: 15 minutes (plus 2-3 hours refrigeration)
Baking: 20 minutes

Cream butter and sugar. Add egg, vanilla, and cinnamon. Beat for 2 to 3 minutes. Add nuts and poppy seeds and beat for another minute. Stir in flour and salt gradually. Chill until dough can be handled to shape into rolls. Make 2 rolls about 2 inches in diameter. Roll in the 2 tablespoons sugar. Wrap the rolls in waxed paper and refrigerate for 2 to 3 hours. Cut into ¼-inch slices. Place cookies on ungreased cookie sheet and bake at 325° about 20 minutes or until cookies start to brown. Cool on racks. Keep in a closed tin.

Betty Garrigues

1 cup butter, softened
1 cup sugar
1 egg
1 teaspoon vanilla
½ teaspoon cinnamon
1½ cups finely chopped nuts
½ cup poppy seeds
2 cups flour
¼ teaspoon salt
2 tablespoons sugar

CHEESECAKE COOKIES

Yield: 16 cookies
Preparation: 25 minutes
Baking: 25 minutes

CRUST:
Mix together sugar, nuts, and flour in a bowl. Stir in butter and mix until light and crumbly. Remove 1 cup of this mixture to be used later as topping. Place remainder in greased 8-inch square pan and press firmly. Bake at 350° for 15 minutes.

FILLING:
Beat softened cream cheese with sugar until smooth. Beat in the egg, lemon juice, milk, and vanilla. Pour this mixture into the baked crust. Top with reserved crumbs and bake at 350° for 25 minutes. Cool thoroughly. Cut into 2-inch squares. Cover and keep refrigerated.

Mary Ellen Smith

CRUST:
1/3 cup brown sugar, packed
½ cup pecans, chopped
1 cup flour
1/3 cup butter, melted

FILLING:
8 ounces cream cheese
¼ cup sugar
1 egg
1 tablespoon lemon juice
2 tablespoons milk
1 teaspoon vanilla

RED RASPBERRY COOKIES

Preparation: 30 minutes (plus refrigeration)
Baking: 8-10 minutes

In a large bowl, cream together butter and sugar until light and fluffy. Add egg and vanilla and beat well. Stir in flour and salt. Mix well to make a smooth dough. If dough is hard to handle, mix with hands. Refrigerate about 2 hours. Lightly grease baking sheets. On a lightly floured board, roll out half of dough to an ⅛-inch thickness. Cut with a 2½-inch cookie cutter. Roll out remaining dough, but cut with a 2½-inch cutter with a hole in the middle. Place on baking sheet. Bake at 375° for 8 to 10 minutes or until lightly browned. Cool approximately 30 minutes. To serve, spread preserves on solid cookie, top with a cut-out cookie, and sprinkle with confectioners' sugar or hazel nuts.

1 cup butter, softened
1½ cups sugar
1 egg
1½ teaspoons vanilla extract
3½ cups flour, stirred before measuring
1 teaspoon salt
½-¾ cup red raspberry preserves
½ cup ground hazelnuts (optional)
Confectioners' sugar

"For Valentine's Day, I use a heart-shaped cookie cutter. A long time favorite of family and friends."
Beverley Brainard Fleming

OLD-FASHIONED RAISIN VANILLA COOKIES

Yield: 6 dozen
Preparation: 1½ hours
Baking: 8-10 minutes
Freeze: Yes

Boil raisins and water together until all the water is absorbed. Remove from heat and cool for 30 minutes. Put butter, sugar, and vanilla in mixing bowl. Cream together for approximately 3 minutes or until light and fluffy. Add eggs, one at a time, beating well after each addition. Add dry ingredients gradually and mix well. Mix in raisin mixture. Drop by teaspoonful into sugar. Roll into balls and place on greased baking sheet. Bake at 375° for 8 to 10 minutes or until nicely browned.

Barbara C. Heiken

1½ cups raisins
1 ½ cups water
1 cup butter, softened
1½ cups sugar
3 eggs
1 teaspoon vanilla
3½ cups flour
1 teaspoon salt
1 teaspoon soda
1 teaspoon baking powder

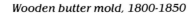

Wooden butter mold, 1800-1850

WARTS

Baking: 13 minutes per sheet

Cream sugar and butter. Add egg, molasses and water. Add flour sifted with soda, salt and spices. Fold in raisins and walnuts. Drop mixture from spoon in small balls onto greased and floured 9 x 13-inch cookie sheets. Bake at 350° for 13 minutes.

½ cup butter or lard
1 cup sugar
1 egg
½ cup molasses
1/3 cup cold water
3 cups flour
1 teaspoon baking soda
½ teaspoon salt
¼ teaspoon cloves
¼ teaspoon ginger
¼ teaspoon mace
1 cup raisins
1 cup walnuts

Russell Ward Nadeau

GRANDMA'S GINGERSNAPS

Yield: 3-4 dozen
Preparation: 15 minutes
Baking: 12 minutes
Freeze: Yes

Cream together shortening and sugar in mixing bowl. Add egg and beat until well blended. To this mixture add molasses, spices, soda, and salt. When blended, add sifted flour. Dough should be rather stiff. Form dough into balls the size of walnuts. Roll each in granulated sugar and place about 2 inches apart on ungreased cookie sheets. Bake at 350° for 12 minutes. Cool on wire racks. If freezing, place in cookie tin with wax paper or plastic wrap.

¾ cup shortening
1 cup sugar
1 egg, beaten
4 tablespoons molasses
1 teaspoon cinnamon
1 teaspoon cloves or allspice
1 teaspoon ginger
2 teaspoons baking soda
Pinch of salt
2 cups sifted flour
Granulated sugar

Julia Hofer

Pewter cream pitcher by John Will, 1752-66

COCONUT POUND CAKE

Preparation: 30 minutes
Baking: 1 hour and 15 minutes

Cream together sugar, butter, and shortening. Beat in eggs, one at a time. Sift together dry ingredients. Add vanilla to milk. Alternate additions of flour and milk to creamed mixture. Beat well after each addition. Add coconut and blend thoroughly. Pour batter into greased and floured tube pan (not a bundt pan). Bake at 350° for 1¼ hour. Do not invert pan to cool. When cool, remove and then invert. Frost with glaze-type icing, if desired. (Note: If unsweetened coconut is used, increase sugar to 2½ cups.)

2 cups sugar
1½ pounds butter
½ cup vegetable shortening
5 eggs
3 cups flour
½ teaspoon salt
½ teaspoon baking powder
1 cup milk
1½ teaspoons vanilla
1 cup shredded sweetened coconut (or 4 ounce package)

Catherine H. Maxwell

FANNIE'S ORANGE CAKE

Serves: 12
Baking: 20-25 minutes
Freeze: Yes

CAKE:
Cream butter. Gradually add sugar and soda mixture; beat thoroughly until light. Add eggs, one at a time, and beat after each addition until mixture is light and fluffy. Slice orange in half and remove seeds. Run orange and raisins through food grinder. Sift together flour, salt, and baking powder; fold into mixture, alternating with buttermilk. Stir in ground raisins and orange. Mix well but do not beat. Put in two well greased and lightly floured 8-inch layer pans. Bake at 350° for 20 to 25 minutes. Let stand 5 minutes before turning out of pan.

ORANGE ICING:
Cream butter until light and fluffy. Beat sugar into it. As it stiffens, add heavy cream. When thickening, add orange juice a little at a time, keeping mixture almost as light and smooth as whipped cream. Spread thickly between layers and on sides and top of cake.

CAKE:
½ cup butter
1 cup sugar mixed with ½ teaspoon soda
2 eggs
1 whole orange, ground
1 cup raisins, ground
2 cups sifted flour
1 teaspoon baking powder
¼ teaspoon salt
½ cup buttermilk

ORANGE ICING:
4 tablespoons butter
1 pound confectioners' sugar
1-3 tablespoons heavy cream
Juice of 1 orange

Geraldine T. Nesbitt

WINTERTHUR CARROT CAKE AND CREAM CHEESE FROSTING

Serves: 12
Baking: 40-50 minutes

CAKE:

Beat eggs and sugar until light and fluffy. Add oil and vanilla and beat well. Sift flour with baking soda, salt, and cinnamon and add to sugar mixture. Beat well. Stir in carrots, raisins, and/or nuts. Pour batter into a greased 9 x 13-inch baking pan. Bake at 300° for 40 to 50 minutes. Cool and spread with Cream Cheese Frosting.

CAKE:

4 eggs
1½ cups sugar
1½ cups oil
2 teaspoons vanilla
2 cups flour
2 teaspoons baking soda
½ teaspoon salt
2 teaspoons cinnamon
2 cups peeled and grated uncooked carrots
1 cup raisins or chopped nuts (or ½ cup each)

CREAM CHEESE FROSTING:

Cream butter and cream cheese. Add sugar and vanilla and beat until smooth. Spread on cooled cake.

CREAM CHEESE FROSTING:

8 ounces cream cheese, softened
½ cup butter, softened
1 pound confectioners' sugar
2 teaspoons vanilla

From **Yuletide at Winterthur.** *Served in the Winterthur Pavilion.*

FRESH APPLE CAKE

Serves: 12-15
Baking: 50 minutes

Put the apples into a large bowl and cover with the sugar. Let stand 10 minutes. Blend oil and eggs into apple mixture. Add dry ingredients and nuts, blending just to mix. Pour into a greased 13 x 9-inch pan and bake at 350° for 50 minutes. Let cool for 10 minutes, then sprinkle granulated sugar over top of cake.

5 apples, peeled and cubed
2 cups sugar
1 cup cooking oil
2 eggs
3 cups sifted flour
2 teaspoons baking soda
½ teaspoon salt
2 teaspoons cinnamon
1 teaspoon nutmeg
1 cup chopped nuts (optional)

Catherine T. Sheats

ALMOND BUTTER CAKE

Serves: 12
Preparation: 2 hours
Baking: 35 minutes

CAKE:

Cream butter; gradually beat in sugar until mixture is light and fluffy and sugar is dissolved. Add eggs, one at a time, beating well after each addition. Combine flour, baking powder, and salt. Add to creamed mixture alternately with milk, beginning and ending with flour mixture. Beat on low speed of electric mixer until just blended. Stir in flavorings. Pour batter into 2 greased and floured 9-inch round cake pans. Bake at 350° for 30 to 35 minutes or until cake tests done. Cool in pans 10 minutes. Remove from pans and complete cooling on wire rack. Spread Butter Cream Frosting between layers and on top and sides of cake.

CAKE:

1 cup butter, softened
2 cups sugar
4 eggs
3 cups flour
2 teaspoons baking powder
1 teaspoon salt
1 cup milk
1 teaspoon vanilla extract
½ teaspoon almond extract
½ teaspoon butter flavoring

BUTTER CREAM FROSTING:

Combine shortening, salt, and extract in a large mixing bowl. Beat at medium speed of electric mixer until blended. Alternately add small amounts of water and confectioners' sugar, beating constantly at low speed until blended.

BUTTER CREAM FROSTING:

1 cup shortening
½ teaspoon salt
1 teaspoon almond extract or butter flavoring
½ cup water
16 ounces confectioners' sugar, sifted

Mary Cash

DATE NUT RING

Serves: 10
Preparation: 20 minutes
Baking: 20-30 minutes
Freeze: Yes

Beat eggs until foamy. Add sugar and mix well. Add milk and stir. Combine flour and baking powder and stir into mixture thoroughly. Stir in dates and nuts. Put into a buttered ring mold (8½ inches in diameter and 2½ inches deep). Bake at 325° for 20 to 30 minutes. Do not overbake; the ring should be chewy. Cool and fill center with sweetened, vanilla-flavored whipped cream or vanilla ice cream.

2 eggs
1 cup sugar
1 tablespoon milk
2 tablespoons flour
1 teaspoon baking powder
1 cup dates, cut fine
1 cup walnuts, chopped
Whipped cream or vanilla ice cream

"A very easy festive dessert. Heat for 3 minutes to serve warm."
Louise Belden

MARY HAMMOND SULLIVAN'S BIRTHDAY CAKE

Serves: 24
Preparation: 40 minutes (plus overnight refrigeration)

CAKE:
Beat egg yolks until fluffy and pale yellow. Cream butter and sugar until light. Add yolks to butter and sugar. Break up macaroons and pour bourbon over them. Let stand after stirring to break up the cookies. Beat the cooled, melted chocolate into the butter mixture. Add vanilla and pecans. Beat egg whites until stiff and fold into the chocolate mixture. Line a tall tube pan with the split lady fingers. Place them around the sides and bottom. Alternate layers of soaked macaroons and chocolate mixture into the lined pan. Layer more lady fingers on the top. Refrigerate overnight.

CAKE:
- 1 dozen eggs, separated
- 1 pound sweet butter
- 2 cups sugar
- ½ pound real coconut macaroons
- ½ pint bourbon
- 4 squares (4 ounces) unsweetened chocolate, melted
- 1 tablespoon vanilla
- 1 cup chopped pecans
- 3 dozen lady fingers, split

WHIPPED CREAM FROSTING:
Whip cream with sugar and vanilla. Before serving, remove cake from refrigerator, preferably to a footed cake plate and cover sides and center with Whipped Cream Frosting.

WHIPPED CREAM FROSTING:
- 2 cups heavy cream
- 3 tablespoons confectioners' sugar
- 1 teaspoon vanilla

Kathryn K. McKenney

SHAKER PINEAPPLE CAKE

Serves: 12
Preparation: 10 minutes
Baking: 30-40 minutes

CAKE:
Beat eggs. Add crushed pineapple, flour, sugar and baking soda. Beat well. Add walnuts and pour batter into ungreased 9 x 13-inch pan. Bake at 350° for 30 to 40 minutes.

CAKE:
- 2 eggs
- 20 ounces crushed pineapple
- 2 cups sifted flour
- 2 cups sugar
- 2 teaspoons baking soda
- 1 cup walnuts

CREAM CHEESE AND BUTTER FROSTING:
Beat until creamy and spread on cake.

CREAM CHEESE AND BUTTER FROSTING:
- ½ pound confectioners' sugar, sifted
- 3 ounces cream cheese
- 1/3 cup butter
- 2 tablespoons cream
- 1 teaspoon vanilla
- ½ cup walnuts

Russell Ward Nadeau

APPLE NUT CAKE

Serves: 12
Preparation: 20 minutes
Baking: 1½ hours

CAKE:
Cream sugar and corn oil. Add eggs, flour, baking soda, vanilla, walnut flavoring, and salt. Beat. In separate bowl mix coconut, nuts, and apples. Fold into creamed mixture. Bake in a greased and floured tube pan at 300° for 1½ hours or until toothpick inserted in center comes out clean. Cool in pan about 20 minutes. Invert cake onto cooling rack and invert again onto plate with top of cake up. Frost if desired.

CAKE:
2 cups sugar
1½ cups corn oil
3 eggs
3 cups flour
1 teaspoon baking soda
1 teaspoon vanilla
½ teaspoon black walnut flavoring
1 teaspoon salt
1 cup unsweetened coconut
½ cup chopped nuts
3 cups chopped and peeled apples

FROSTING:
Combine all frosting ingredients in saucepan and bring to boil over medium heat. Cook for 3 minutes. Pour over cooled cake.

FROSTING:
¼ pound butter
¼ cup milk
1 cup brown sugar

Ruth Lee

WALNUT CAKE

Serves: 8-12
Preparation: 15 minutes
Baking: 25 minutes

Beat 6 eggs and 1 cup of sugar together until light. Add walnuts, flour, and baking powder. Pour mixture into two lightly greased layer cake pans. Bake at 350° for 25 minutes. Whipped cream may be used between layers and as icing. Serve very thin slices.

6 eggs
1 cup sugar
1 pound shelled walnuts, ground fine
1 tablespoon flour
2 tablespoons baking powder
Whipped cream (optional)

Mrs. Robert E. Kelly, Jr.

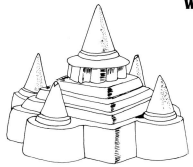

Salt-glazed stoneware jelly mold, 1760-80

ORANGE CAKE

Serves: 10-12
Preparation: 30 minutes
Baking: 1 hour

Add vinegar to milk to sour it. Cream butter with sugar and add beaten eggs. Chop rind of oranges with raisins. Add sour milk to butter mixture, then add flour, salt, baking soda, rind and raisins, vanilla, and lemon extract. Bake in a buttered tube pan at 325° for 1 hour.

Mix squeezed juice of oranges and sugar. Leave cake in pan and pour juice mixture over cake. Let stand until juice is absorbed before putting on cake plate.

4 teaspoons vinegar
1½ cups milk
1 cup butter
2 cups sugar
4 eggs, beaten
Rind of oranges
2 cups raisins
2 teaspoons baking soda
4 cups flour
2/3 teaspoon salt
2 teaspoons vanilla
2 teaspoons lemon extract
Juice of 2 oranges
1 cup sugar

"It took me three years to obtain the recipe from my husband's aunt's cook. Worth the effort."
  Mrs. John Learned

TIA MARIA ALMOND TORTE

Yield: 1 9-inch cake
Baking: 1 hour

CAKE:
Beat egg whites until foamy. Gradually beat in ¼ cup sugar until stiff. In separate bowl, beat yolks with ½ cup of sugar to a pale lemon color. Add almonds, salt, baking powder, and ¼ cup of Tia Maria. Mix well and fold into egg whites. Pour mixture into greased 9-inch springform pan. Bake at 300° for 60 minutes. Loosen sides of cake with sharp knife. Cool 5 minutes. Remove cake from pan, turn over, and let cool. Drizzle cake with ¼ cup of liqueur before frosting.

FROSTING:
Melt chocolate in top of double boiler. Cool slightly. Gradually stir in butter and liqueur mixture. Mix well. Chill until spreadable.

CAKE:
5 eggs, separated (plus 2 yolks)
¾ cup sugar
7½ ounces unblanched almonds, finely ground
Pinch salt
½ teaspoon baking powder
½ cup Tia Maria (or other coffee-flavored liqueur)

FROSTING:
6 ounces semisweet chocolate bits
¼ cup sweet butter, cut into pieces
2 teaspoons instant coffee dissolved in ¼ cup Tia Maria

Alison Keeling

FORGOTTEN TORTE

Serves: 8
Preparation: 15 minutes
Baking: Overnight
Freeze: Yes

Beat egg whites until frothy. Add salt and cream of tartar. Beat until very stiff, then add sugar gradually beating continuously. Add vanilla. Spread in a greased springform pan, pie pan, or individual tart pans. Heat oven to 450°. Turn heat off and put torte in oven leaving overnight or several hours. To serve, fill with any fruit topped with whipped cream or with peppermint ice cream topped with hot chocolate sauce.

5 egg whites
¼ teaspoon salt
½ teaspoon cream of tartar
1½ cups sugar
1 teaspoon vanilla

Joyce Smedley

BAKED ALASKA

Serves: 4
Preparation: 10 minutes
Baking: 4 minutes

Place slices of pound cake on ungreased cookie sheet. Add vanilla and salt to the egg whites and beat until stiff, adding sugar slowly. Place two scoops of well-chilled ice cream onto each piece of pound cake. Mold into small compact "towers" on each piece of cake. Using a wide spatula, quickly paint meringue all around each tower, completely covering ice cream and cake. (If there is a hole in the meringue, the ice cream will start to melt and flow through that hole.) Place in 450° oven for 3 to 4 minutes until meringue is lightly browned. Using a spatula, place individual servings on each dessert plate.

4 slices of pound cake
1 teaspoon vanilla
½ teaspoon salt
5 egg whites
¾ cup granulated sugar
8 scoops of your favorite ice cream

Joyce Hill Stoner

Earthenware muffin pan or jelly mold, 1800-1875

CHERRIES JUBILEE

Serves: 6
Cooking: 10 minutes

Combine lemon juice, sugar, and cherry syrup in a saucepan or chafing dish over high heat, stirring constantly until mixture is well blended. Gradually sift cornstarch into mixture, stirring constantly until sauce is thick and clear. Reduce heat. Add cherries, lemon peel, almond extract, and brandy to mixture. Simmer for 2 minutes, stirring constantly. Remove from heat but keep warm if not used immediately. If desired, pour another ¼ cup of cherry brandy over mixture before serving. Ignite without stirring. When flame burns out, serve over ice cream or cake a la mode.

John H. Meszaros

2 teaspoons lemon juice
1/3 cup sugar
1 cup cherry syrup (from canned cherries)
2-3 tablespoons cornstarch
1½ cups canned bing cherries, pitted and drained
¼ teaspoon grated lemon peel
¼ teaspoon almond extract
¼ cup cherry brandy

PARFAIT AU GRAND MARNIER

Serves: 4
Preparation: 15 minutes (plus 4 hours freezing)

Combine egg yolks and sugar; beat until foamy. Add Grand Marnier. Whip cream and fold into egg mixture. Beat egg whites until stiff peaks form. Fold gently into egg mixture. Pour into 9 x 5 x 3-inch loaf pan and freeze for 4 hours.

Sylvia Bisbe

2 eggs, separated
1/3 cup sugar
4 tablespoons Grand Marnier liqueur
½ pint heavy whipping cream

Silver tankard made by Paul Revere, 1772

CLASSIC CHEESECAKE

Serves: 12
Preparation: 20 minutes
Baking: 2 hours (plus 3 hours for cooling)
Freeze: Yes

Butter an 8 x 3-inch cake pan and sprinkle with graham cracker crumbs, shaking until bottom and sides are coated. Shake out excess crumbs and set pan aside. Place cream cheese, sugar, lemon juice, lemon rind, and vanilla in the large bowl of an electric mixer and beat at low speed. Add eggs one at a time. Gradually increase speed to high. Continue beating until mixture is smooth. Pour and scrape batter into the prepared pan and shake gently to level the mixture. Set the pan inside a slightly larger pan and pour boiling water into the outer pan to a depth of ½ inch. Do not let edge of cheesecake pan touch rim of larger pan. Bake at 250° for 90 minutes. Increase to 275° for 30 minutes more. Turn off heat and let cake sit in oven for 1 hour. Lift cake out of the water bath and place on a rack; let stand 2 hours. Invert serving plate over cake and carefully turn upside down so that cake comes out crumb side up. Garnish with fruit.

Ursula H. Bright

½ cup graham cracker crumbs
2 pounds (4 8-ounce packages) cream cheese at room temperature
1¾ cups sugar
Juice and grated rind of 1 lemon
1 teaspoon vanilla
4 eggs
Strawberries, blueberries, or other fruit for garnish

CHEESE TORTE

Serves: 10-12
Preparation: 30 minutes
Baking: 1 hour (plus refrigeration)

Mix crumbs with ½ cup of sugar. Add cinnamon and butter. Set aside ¾ cup crumb mixture. Butter 9-inch springform pan. Press remaining crumb mixture evenly on bottom and sides; any leftover crumbs may be added to the reserved 1¾ cup. Beat eggs with remaining 1 cup sugar until light. Add salt, lemon, and vanilla. Stir in milk and flour. Push cottage cheese through sieve or food mill and add to mixture. Pour into pan and top with reserved crumb mixture. Bake at 325° for 1 hour. Turn off heat and let torte stand in oven 1 hour or more. Refrigerate.

1 6-ounce package zwieback, crushed
1½ cups granulated sugar
1½ teaspoons cinnamon
½ cup plus 2 tablespoons butter, melted
4 eggs
Dash of salt
Juice and grated rind of 1 lemon
1 teaspoon vanilla extract
1 can evaporated milk
1½ pounds small curd cottage cheese
¼ cup flour

"This cheesecake-like dessert becomes an extra special treat when served with Cherry Heering liqueur."
Tilly Maassen

CREAM CHEESE PIE

Serves: 12
Preparation: 30 minutes
Baking: 30 minutes
Freeze: Yes

PIE:
Line 9-inch springform pan or pie plate with crackers that have been mixed with melted butter; set aside. In large bowl combine eggs, sugar, cream cheese, and lemon juice. Beat at moderate speed until smooth, approximately 3 to 5 minutes. Add vanilla. Gently pour into pie crust. Bake at 350° for 25 minutes.

PIE:
12 crushed graham crackers (double size)
6 tablespoons butter, melted
2 eggs
¾ cup sugar
1 pound cream cheese
1 teaspoon lemon juice
1 teaspoon vanilla

TOPPING:
Mix sour cream, sugar and vanilla and spread over pie. Return to oven for 5 minutes (this does not brown). Garnish each serving with a thin lemon slice.

TOPPING:
1 pint sour cream
2 tablespoons sugar
1 teaspoon vanilla
Lemon slices

"Very rich, so servings should be small."
  Mrs. W. Ellis Preston

DRUNKEN PRUNES

Serves: 6-8
Preparation: 15 minutes (plus 24 hours soaking time)
Cooking: 30 minutes (plus 3 days refrigeration)

Soak prunes for 24 hours in 2 cups of red port. Add 1 cup of sugar, 2 additional cups of port, and ½ of a split vanilla bean. Cook in covered enamel saucepan over low heat for about 30 minutes. When cool, refrigerate in a covered glass container. The prunes are ready to eat in 3 days. To serve, place several prunes in each glass dish and cover with whipped cream. Sprinkle with powdered macaroons and decorate with candied violets. Serve with additional macaroons or crisp sugar cookies.

1 box large pitted prunes (about 34)
4 cups good red port
1 cup sugar
½ vanilla bean
Candied violets
Powdered macaroons
Whipped cream

"These keep in the icebox indefinitely and make a wonderful rich dessert for unexpected guests."
  Susan Gardener

PLUM PUDDING

Serves: 18
Cooking: 9 hours (begin 1 week in advance)

Mix together suet, crumbs, flour, spices, salt, and sugar. Add fruit and, after this, eggs, milk, and brandy. Place pudding mixture in center of a clean, wet, well floured cloth approximately 20 inches square. Beginning with one corner of cloth, gather folds together above pudding; tie string around cloth just above pudding, leaving extra room for swelling. Place in pudding steamer and steam for 6 hours. Hang for a week in a cool dry place. Steam for 3 hours on day it is served. Dot with blanched almonds. Garnish with a sprig of holly on top; douse with brandy and ignite. Serve with Lemon Sauce for Plum Pudding, Christmas Pudding Sauce, or a traditional hard sauce.

1 pound suet, chopped fine
½ pound bread crumbs
¾ pound flour
1 nutmeg, grated
½ teaspoon cinnamon
½ teaspoon cloves
1 teaspoon salt
1 pound brown sugar
2 pounds seedless raisins
1 pound dried currants
¼ pound candied orange peel
8 eggs, slightly beaten
½ cup cold milk
4 ounces brandy
½ cup shelled almonds, blanched and chopped fine

"An old English recipe."
  Mrs. John Learned

LEMON SAUCE FOR PLUM PUDDING

Preparation: 5 minutes
Cooking: 10 minutes

Melt butter and sugar until smooth; add cream and scald. Pour in thin stream over beaten egg yolks, stirring constantly. Continue cooking until it thickens into a light custard. Add nutmeg, lemon juice, and vanilla. Be careful not to overheat or it will curdle. Whisk in liquor. Serve warm or cold.

1 pound butter
2 cups sugar
1 cup light cream
2 egg yolks
½ teaspoon nutmeg
Juice of 1 lemon
1 tablespoon vanilla
½ cup sherry, port or rum

"A du Pont family recipe."
  Annie Jones

Brass nutcracker, 1750-1800

CHRISTMAS PUDDING SAUCE

Preparation: 15 minutes

Mix the beaten egg with the sugar, flour, and salt. Add to the scalded milk and mix in vanilla. Heat until thick. Pour over fig pudding or plum pudding.

1 egg, beaten
1 cup sugar
1 tablespoon flour
Dash of salt
1 cup milk, scalded
1 teaspoon vanilla

Mrs. William Innes Homer

ORANGES IN WINE SAUCE

Serves: 4
Preparation: 10 minutes
Cooking: 10 minutes

Bring first 6 ingredients to boil in a saucepan. Boil hard until reduced by half. Remove cloves. Pour boiling sauce over sectioned oranges. Refrigerate until well chilled. Serve with butter cookies.

1 cup dry red wine
1 cup water
¾ cup sugar
2 lemon slices
3 cloves
½ teaspoon cinnamon
4 oranges, sectioned

"An excellent dessert after luncheon or after a rich meal. Especially nice in summer."
  Isabelle H. Bow

FRUIT FANTASY

Preparation: 30 minutes (plus refrigeration)

Grind together dates, raisins, figs, and prunes. Mix with walnuts, coconut, and orange rind. Press mixture tightly into an 8-inch square pan lined with aluminum foil. Chill a few days in the refrigerator before slicing for serving. Slice ¼-inch wide or thinner, then cut lengthwise into pieces.

1 pound dates
1 pound raisins
1 pound figs
½ pound prunes
1 pound English walnuts
  before shelling or 4½
  ounces shelled
1 cup grated coconut
Rind of 1 orange, grated

"This recipe has been known to keep under refrigeration for a year."
  Mrs. Antonio Alvarez

BEEHIVE PEACHES

Serves: 8
Preparation: 25 minutes
Baking: 30-40 minutes

PEACHES:
Roll pie crust into oblong and cut into strips. Starting at bottom, wrap strips around peach until entire peach is covered. Pat to seal the edges. Place in pan and bake at 400° for 30 to 40 minutes. Serve hot. The peach skin disappears; each guest removes stone and fills hollow with Hard Sauce passed in a separate bowl.

HARD SAUCE:
Cream butter. Add unbeaten egg and mix well. Gradually work in sugar. Flavor with vanilla or brandy. Pile in serving bowl and sprinkle with nutmeg.

PEACHES:
Double pie crust recipe
8 perfect, fresh peaches

HARD SAUCE:
4 tablespoons butter
1 egg, unbeaten
2 cups confectioners' sugar
1 teaspoon vanilla or brandy
Nutmeg

"Peaches can be prepared in morning. Put them in oven to bake while you are eating dinner."
Nancy Lennig Bayard

BRENDA'S MONKEY CAKES

Serves: 2-4
Preparation: 10 minutes
Baking: 20 minutes

Put sugar and cinnamon in tightly covered container and shake well to mix. Take biscuits from can and separate. Shake each biscuit in cinnamon-sugar mixture to coat well and place in greased 9-inch cake pan. In a small pan, melt butter and brown sugar until well mixed. Dribble over coated biscuits in pan. Bake at 350° for 20 minutes. Serve warm.
Company version: Quadruple all ingredients. Cut biscuits into quarters before dusting with cinnamon-sugar mixture. Place in greased tube pan. Pour brown sugar-butter mixture over all. Bake at 350° for 30 minutes.

1 can refrigerator biscuits (10 in a can)
1 cup granulated white sugar
2 tablespoons cinnamon
½ cup brown sugar, firmly packed
¼ cup butter

"Great munchy with hot or cold beverage."
Isabelle H. Bow

RUM PUDDING

Serves: 6-8
Preparation: 10 minutes
(plus 4 hours refrigeration)

Beat egg yolks and add sugar. Whip cream until stiff. Dissolve gelatin in wine and add with rum to whipped cream. Fold mixture together and chill at least 4 hours. Add berries, apricots, or any fruit. Can be chilled in individual compotes or bowl.

Jane Figgins

6 egg yolks
1 cup sugar
2 cups heavy cream
1½ tablespoons gelatin
4 ounces white wine
3 ounces rum
Fresh fruit

RASPBERRY MOUSSE

Serves: 8-10
Preparation: 30 minutes
Freeze: Yes (up to 2 weeks)

Put egg whites in mixing bowl with sugar and thawed raspberries. Whip for 15 minutes. Add lemon juice and salt. Whip cream to form soft peaks. Fold into raspberry mixture. Pour into 3-quart glass dish. Top with whipped cream and nuts, if desired. To freeze, omit topping with whipped cream and nuts until time to serve.

Mrs. Robert E. Putney

2 egg whites
¾ cup sugar
1 10-ounce box frozen raspberries
1 tablespoon lemon juice
Dash of salt
1 cup heavy cream, whipped

HEIRLOOM GINGERBREAD

Serves: 8
Preparation: 15 minutes
Baking: 30 minutes

Combine flour, sugar, ginger, and cinnamon; cut in shortening. Reserve ¼ cup for topping. Add egg to remaining flour mixture and stir in molasses. Dissolve soda and salt in buttermilk. Add to molasses mixture and pour into greased 8-inch square pan. Sprinkle the reserved topping over batter. Bake at 350° for approximately 30 minutes.

1½ cups flour
1 cup sugar
½ teaspoon ground ginger
1 teaspoon cinnamon
½ cup butter or shortening
1 egg, slightly beaten
2 tablespoons molasses
1 teaspoon soda
Scant teaspoon salt
1 cup buttermilk

"Served hot, this makes a yummy coffee cake. Served cold, it is a velvety and delicious dessert cake."
  Mrs. Antonio Alvarez

STRAWBERRY PANCAKES

Serves: 6-8
Preparation: 45 minutes

Sift flour, baking soda, salt, and sugar together. Set aside. Beat egg, milk, and vinegar together and combine with flour mixture. Stir until smooth. Make pancakes in desired size. Set aside. Meanwhile mix together cream cheese, sugar, lemon juice, and almond extract until smooth; spread on pancakes and roll. To serve at once, brush with melted butter and reheat at 300° until warm. Pancakes may also be frozen, then heated in melted butter at 300° for approximately 10 minutes. Serve with sweetened fresh strawberries or thawed, undrained strawberries and garnish with whipped cream, if desired.

1 cup sifted flour
½ teaspoon baking soda
¼ teaspoon salt
2 tablespoons sugar
1 egg
1 cup milk
2 tablespoons vinegar
10 ounces fresh sliced strawberries (frozen may be substituted)
8 ounces cream cheese, softened
¼ cup sugar
2 tablespoons lemon juice
¼ teaspoon almond extract
Butter
Heavy cream, whipped and lightly sweetened (optional)

Joyce McClung

FRESH ORANGE MOUSSE WITH TOASTED ALMONDS

Serves: 8
Preparation: 30 minutes (plus 6 hours refrigeration)

Soften gelatin in cold water for 15 minutes. While soaking, put sugar, orange rind, and water into a pan and boil for 1 minute. Dissolve gelatin in syrup. Add orange and lemon juices. Refrigerate until mousse begins to thicken, approximately 30 minutes. Fold in whipped cream. Pile high into sherbert glasses and return to refrigerator for 6 hours. Garnish with toasted almonds.

1 tablespoon gelatin
¼ cup cold water
1 cup sugar
3 tablespoons freshly grated orange rind
½ cup boiling water
1 cup freshly squeezed strained orange juice
¼ cup freshly squeezed lemon juice
¾ cup cream, whipped
1 cup toasted slivered almonds

Mrs. Kathleen Swank

APPLE FRITTERS

Serves: 4-6
Preparation: 1 hour

Pare, core, and cut the apples into thick slices. Mix sugar and 2 tablespoons brandy or rum and combine with apple slices; set aside for ½ hour. Make a batter with the other ingredients, except the egg whites. Gently fold beaten egg whites into batter. Dip each slice of apple in batter. Fry in deep hot fat until delicately browned on both sides. Remove with skimmer, and drain on a towel. Sprinkle with confectioners' sugar, and glaze under the broiler. Serve very hot.

4 medium-sized Delicious apples
2 tablespoons confectioners' sugar
4 tablespoons brandy or rum
3 ounces flour
1 pinch salt
1 tablespoon butter, melted
3 egg whites, beaten until stiff
2 tablespoons beer
2 tablespoons warm water

Winterthur Archives

SOUR CREAM POUND CAKE

Serves: 12-16
Preparation: 30 minutes
Baking: 1½ hours
Freeze: Yes

Generously grease and lightly flour tube pan. Add baking soda to sour cream and set aside. Cream butter and sugar. Add egg yolks, one at a time, mixing well after each addition. Alternately mix in sour cream and flour. Mix well after each addition. Add vanilla. Beat egg whites until stiff and fold in last. Pour into prepared tube pan. Bake at 300° for 1½ hours. Cool in pan 30 minutes before turning onto wire rack. When completely cooled, store in tightly covered container or wrap in plastic wrap. Better if made the day before serving.

3 cups flour, sifted
1 cup sour cream
½ pound butter, softened
3 cups sugar
6 eggs, separated
1 teaspoon baking soda
1 teaspoon vanilla

Mrs. Charles G. Rivers, Jr.

SHORTBREAD

Serves: 16
Baking: 45 minutes-1 hour

Put butter and sugar into a bowl. Work together until free of lumps. Gradually add 1 cup of flour. Turn onto table and knead in second cup of flour. After kneading well, press ½-inch deep into 8-inch square shallow pan. Mark with fork. Bake at 300° for 45 minutes to an hour. Cut into squares or diamonds.

½ pound butter
¾ cup sugar
2 cups flour

Agnes Paterson

Chocolate

Josiah Wedgwood was one of the most inventive English potters of the eighteenth century. In the mid-eighteenth century, his improvements on the traditional Staffordshire creamware set a new standard of quality and laid the foundation for his success. When Wedgwood's new cream-colored ware won royal patronage around 1765, it was named "Queen's Ware." Queen's ware was more durable than tin-glazed earthenware or salt-glazed stoneware, and it had a clean, fine-textured body. In order to appeal to those who were accustomed to setting their tables with expensive imported porcelain, Wedgwood sold queen's ware at high prices. The range of decoration on queen's ware includes molding, piercing, colored glazing, transfer printing, and hand painting with enamel.

Irish Whiskey Chocolate Cake is served here on creamware plates with a hand-painted enamel bellflower and leaf border, made in Staffordshire, 1771-1810. The table in the Du Pont Dining Room also displays champagne glasses of leaded glass cut with flutes, fans, and strawberry diamond patterns, made in England, Ireland, or Pittsburgh, Pennsylvania, 1800-1835; silver forks in the King's pattern made by various New York makers, 1800-1845; steel-plated knives in early George III style, probably made in England; and green and white linens once used in the home of Henry Francis du Pont.

IRISH WHISKEY CHOCOLATE CAKE

Serves: 12
Preparation: 20 minutes
Baking: 30 minutes

CAKE:
Preheat oven to 350°. Butter and flour two 9-inch layer cake pans. Combine all cake ingredients together in large bowl. Blend well, then beat at medium mixer speed for 2 minutes. Pour into prepared pans. Bake 30 minutes or until cake tests done. Do not underbake. Cool in pans 10 minutes. Remove from pans and finish cooling on racks. Split layers in half horizontally.

FILLING:
To make filling, combine cream, cocoa, sugar, and vanilla in large mixing bowl. Beat until stiff. Fold in whiskey. Spread one cup of filling between each layer, stacking layers, and over top of cake. Keep cake chilled. Serve cold. Walnuts can be sprinkled between each layer before adding filling.

Cheryl K. Gibbs

CAKE:
1 18 ½-ounce chocolate cake mix with pudding
3 eggs
½ cup Irish whiskey
½ cup cold water
1/3 cup oil

FILLING:
1 pint heavy cream
1/3 cup unsweetened cocoa
½ cup confectioners' sugar
1 teaspoon vanilla
½ cup Irish whiskey
½ cup chopped walnuts (optional)

PENNSYLVANIA GERMAN CHOCOLATE CAKE

Serves: 12
Preparation: 20 minutes
Baking: 35 minutes

CAKE:
Butter and flour a 9 x 13-inch baking pan. Preheat oven to 350°. In a large mixing bowl, stir together the cocoa, butter, and water until the butter is melted. Mix in the sugar. Sift together the flour, salt, and baking soda. Add the dry ingredients to the cocoa mixture alternately with the buttermilk, beating after each addition. Add the vanilla and egg to the batter and beat 2 minutes on medium speed. Pour batter into cake pan. Bake 35 minutes or until a wooden toothpick inserted in center comes out clean.

BROILED COCONUT TOPPING:
Mix all ingredients together. Spread on warm cake. Broil until golden and bubbly.

Lenore K. Holt

CAKE:
½ cup cocoa
½ cup butter
¾ cup boiling water
2 cups granulated sugar
2 cups flour
½ teaspoon salt
1½ teaspoons baking soda
1 cup buttermilk
1 teaspoon vanilla
1 egg, slightly beaten

BROILED COCONUT TOPPING:
6 tablespoons butter, melted
1 cup brown sugar
1/3 cup milk
1 teaspoon vanilla
1½ cups coconut and/or finely chopped nuts or rolled oats

SECRET CAKE

Serves: 15-18
Preparation: 30 minutes
Baking: 15-20 minutes

CAKE:

To make cake, place flour and sugar in a large mixing bowl and set aside. Put butter, shortening, water and cocoa in a saucepan and let come to a boil, thickening slightly. Pour over flour and sugar and mix well. Add to this mixture the buttermilk, eggs, vanilla, salt, and soda; mix well. Pour batter into buttered and lightly floured 11 x 16 x 1-inch pan or cookie sheet; cake batter will be on the runny side and will pour easily into pan. Bake at 400° for 15 to 20 minutes.

CAKE:
2 cups flour
2 cups sugar
¼ pound butter
½ cup shortening
1 cup water
3½ tablespoons cocoa (or more to taste)
½ cup buttermilk
2 eggs
1 teaspoon vanilla
½ teaspoon salt
1 teaspoon baking soda

ICING:

While cake is baking, prepare icing. Place butter, cocoa, and buttermilk in same pan used in the beginning and boil until slightly thickened, stirring constantly. Remove from stove and add confectioners' sugar, vanilla, and nuts, mixing well. Ice cake as soon as it is removed from the oven.

ICING:
¼ pound butter
3½ tablespoons cocoa
1/3 cup buttermilk
1 pound confectioners' sugar
1 teaspoon vanilla
1 cup chopped nuts (optional)

"This is a delicious fudgy cake and is served in the pan in which it is baked."
Mrs. Gary L. Mitchell

CHOCOLATE MOUSSE CAKE

Serves: 8
Preparation: 1 hour
Cooking: 35 minutes

Melt the chocolate and butter in a saucepan. Add sugar gradually, and the egg yolks one at a time; beat for three minutes at high speed. In a separate bowl, beat egg whites until stiff (add a little sugar to help hold the peaks). Fold egg whites slowly into the chocolate batter with a spatula. Pour only three-quarters of the batter into an ungreased springform pan. Bake at 325° for 35 minutes. Let cake cool and fall. Run knife around edge and remove frame. Pour the remaining batter on top and chill. Serve with whipped cream and garnish with chocolate shavings.

7 ounces semisweet chocolate
¼ pound butter
1 cup sugar
7 eggs, separated
Heavy cream, whipped
Chocolate shavings

Diane Hamilton Sanders

WASHINGTON CHOCOLATE CAKE

Serves: 10-12
Preparation: 12 minutes
Baking: 30 minutes

Preheat oven to 375°. Measure dry ingredients, including cinnamon if desired, into an 8-inch square or 9-inch round baking pan and stir together. Measure in liquid ingredients and stir well. Bake 30 minutes or until center is puffed and sides begin to pull away from edge of pan. Cool before cutting. Cake does not turn out of pan easily, so it should be cut into squares and lifted out with a spatula. Attractive when sprinkled with sifted powdered sugar.

"A quick and easy cake to accompany fresh fruit or ice cream."
Mrs. A. Atwater Kent, Jr.

1 cup sugar
1½ cups flour
1/3 cup cocoa
1 teaspoon baking soda
½ teaspoon salt
2 teaspoons vanilla
½ cup oil
1 cup cold water
1 teaspoon cinnamon (optional)

MOCHA ROLL

Serves: 8
Preparation: 20 minutes (plus 1 hour refrigeration)
Baking: 15 minutes
Freeze: Yes

Butter an 11 x 17-inch jelly roll pan and line with wax paper. Butter again. Melt the chocolate in the coffee, add mocha extract and vanilla; mix until smooth. Preheat oven to 350°. Beat egg yolks and add the sugar, beating until thick and light. Stir in the chocolate mixture. Fold in the egg whites. Spread evenly in the prepared pan and bake 15 minutes. (Do not overbake; cake should be fairly moist.) Cover with a damp cloth and refrigerate for 1 hour. Sprinkle confectioners' sugar on a piece of wax paper and turn cake out on it. Peel paper away and spread with whipped cream. Roll up like a jelly roll and chill. Can be frozen up to several weeks.

Peggy Frankenburg

6 ounces German sweet chocolate
3 tablespoons brewed coffee
1 teaspoon mocha extract
1 teaspoon vanilla
5 egg yolks
2/3 cup sugar
5 egg whites, stiffly beaten
½ cup confectioners' sugar
1 cup heavy cream, whipped

Earthenware knife rest with tin-enamel glaze, 1720-60

BLACK COCOA CAKE

Serves: 12-16
Baking: 30 to 40 minutes.

CAKE:
Blend all dry ingredients in a large bowl. Add remaining ingredients and mix well. Bake at 350° in greased and floured tube pan for 30 to 40 minutes.

CAKE:
2 cups flour
2 cups sugar
1 cup cocoa
1 teaspoon baking powder
2 teaspoons baking soda
½ cup melted butter
1 cup milk
1 cup hot black coffee
2 eggs, beaten
1 teaspoon vanilla

ICING:
Cream butter and sugar; blend in egg white. Add remaining liquid ingredients, adding more if needed to adjust taste and consistency.

ICING:
¼ pound butter
3 cups confectioners' sugar
1 egg white
1 tablespoon buttermilk
¼ teaspoon Triple Sec (or to taste)
⅛ teaspoon almond extract (or to taste)

Mario Buatta

CHOCOLATE MOUSSE

Serves: 10
Preparation: 30 minutes (plus refrigeration)

Melt chocolate in double boiler. When melted add butter. After butter is melted, remove from heat. Add sugar and mix well until smooth. Add 10 egg yolks to mixture and beat well. Beat egg whites until stiff. Add to mixture and mix until stiff. Pour into compotes and refrigerate overnight. Serve with whipped cream and fresh sliced strawberries.

½ pound semisweet chocolate
2 tablespoons butter
10 tablespoons of sugar
10 eggs, separated
Heavy cream, whipped
Fresh strawberries, sliced

Winterthur Archives

DOUBLE CHOCOLATE CHARLOTTE

Serves: 12
Preparation: 1 hour
Baking: 30 minutes (plus 4 hours refrigeration)
Freeze: Yes

BROWNIE CRUST:

Grease 9 x 9 x 2-inch pan. Cut wax paper to fit bottom and up two sides. Grease and flour paper. To make crust, melt butter and chocolate over low heat. Remove from heat and beat in sugar and eggs. Sift flour, baking powder, and salt onto wax paper. Stir into chocolate mixture until smooth and add vanilla. Pour into prepared pan. Bake at 350° for 35 minutes. Cool on wire rack. Invert onto cookie sheet and peel off paper. Slice brownie horizontally to make two thin layers. Cut a 7-inch circle for one layer and fit it, cut side up, into the bottom of an 8-inch souffle dish. Cut remaining layer into three strips. Arrange around edge to form a lining.

FILLING:

To make filling, melt chocolate with coffee in top of double boiler. Remove from heat and stir in liqueur. Beat egg yolks until thick. Stir into chocolate mixture until well blended and pour into large bowl. Allow to cool. Beat egg whites in small bowl until stiff but not dry. Beat ½ cup of the cream until stiff. Fold cream, then egg whites, into chocolate mixture until no streaks of white remain. Spoon into crust. Trim edges level with filling. Refrigerate at least 4 hours. To serve, loosen around edge with spatula. Turn upside down on serving dish. Whip remaining cream until stiff and decorate the Charlotte. Garnish with chocolate curls.

BROWNIE CRUST:
- 1/3 cup butter
- 2 squares unsweetened chocolate
- 1 cup sugar
- 2 eggs, well beaten
- ¾ cup sifted flour
- ½ teaspoon baking powder
- ¼ teaspoon salt
- 1 teaspoon vanilla

FILLING:
- 2 12-ounce packages chocolate chips
- ½ cup strong brewed coffee
- ½ cup coffee liqueur
- 3 eggs, separated
- 1 cup heavy cream
- Chocolate curls

"A spectacular and delicious dessert well worth the trouble."
    Louise C. Belden

QUICK POTS DE CREME

Serves: 6
Preparation: 5 minutes (plus refrigeration)

Put all ingredients in blender. Blend on high for 1 minute. Pour into 6 pots or demitasse cups. Chill. Garnish with crystallized violet in center.

- ¾ cup milk, heated to boiling point
- 1 cup semisweet chocolate morsels
- 1 egg
- 2 tablespoons sugar
- 2 tablespoons rum or liqueur (Cointreau, Amaretto, etc.)

Mrs. William C. Lindsay

FRENCH SILK PIE I

Serves: 6
Preparation: 15-20 minutes
(plus 2-3 hours
refrigeration)

Cream butter and sugar together with electric beater at slow speed. Blend in melted chocolate and vanilla. Add eggs one at a time, beating at medium speed 4 minutes after each egg (total, 12 minutes). Pour into pie crust. Chill 2 to 3 hours. Top each serving with whipped cream and shavings of bitter chocolate for decoration.

¾ cup butter
1¾ cups confectioners' sugar, sifted
1½ squares unsweetened chocolate, melted
1½ teaspoons vanilla
3 eggs
1 8-inch butter-flavored pie crust
Whipped cream
Bitter chocolate shavings

"A delicate chocolate flavor, very smooth and rich."
Lucie Frederick

FRENCH SILK PIE II

Serves: 8
Preparation: 30 minutes (plus refrigeration)
Baking: 10 minutes for crust

CRUST:
Crush wafers. Add melted butter. Press into 9-inch pie pan. Bake at 350° for 10 minutes. Cool.

FILLING:
Whip butter and sugar together thoroughly. Add vanilla and melted chocolate; beat. Add eggs, one at a time, beating well after each egg. Fold in pecans. Turn into crust. Chill.

CRUST:
25 vanilla wafers
¼ cup butter, melted

FILLING:
¾ cup butter
1 cup sugar
1 teaspoon vanilla
2 squares unsweetened chocolate, melted
3 eggs
½ cup pecans

Bonnie Korengel

Blue and white Chinese export porcelain plate, 1750-80

CHOCOLATE PECAN PIE

Serves: 8-9
Baking: 1 hour

Place sheet of foil in bottom and up sides of pie crust. Weight with uncooked beans and bake at 450° for 12 minutes. Reduce heat to 400°; remove foil and beans and continue baking 3 minutes longer. Melt chocolate and butter in top of double boiler over moderate heat until melted. Remove from heat and stir to blend. Set aside and cool. Beat eggs in bowl with electric mixer. Add sugar and syrup, beating just to mix. Add vanilla, rum, melted chocolate and pecans. Mix well. Pour into partially baked crust and bake 40 to 50 minutes at 350°. Top should feel soft to the touch and middle should shimmy; as filling cools it will firm. If top begins to brown too much, cover lightly with sheet of foil. After removing from oven, place on rack to cool. Serve warm or refrigerate and serve cold with whipped cream.

1 deep 9-inch pie crust
2 ounces unsweetened chocolate
4 tablespoons butter
4 large eggs
¾ cup sugar
1¼ cups dark corn syrup
1 teaspoon vanilla
2½ tablespoons dark rum
8 ounces pecan halves

Pat Reeser

CHOCOLATE ALMOND CREAM PIE

Serves: 6
Preparation: 15-20 minutes (plus refrigeration)
Baking: 8 minutes for crust

CRUST:
Combine graham cracker crumbs and sugar and stir in butter until blended. Pack firmly into a 9-inch pie pan bringing crumbs evenly up to rim. Bake at 350° for 8 minutes and allow to cool.

CRUST:
1¼ cups graham cracker crumbs
3 tablespoons sugar
1/3 cup butter, melted

FILLING:
Melt chocolate bars in top of double boiler. Add marshmallows, a few at a time, stirring until all are melted. Mix in milk, remove from stove and allow to cool 30 to 45 minutes. Beat cream, fold into cooled mixture, and pour into graham cracker crust. Refrigerate for several hours and serve.

FILLING:
5-1.45 ounce chocolate bars with almonds
16 regular-sized marshmallows
½ cup milk
½ pint whipping cream

"If you wish, decorate top with almonds or with additional whipped cream."
    Betty Jean Bolton

CHOCOLATE LOG

Serves: 6-8
Preparation: 1 hour
Baking: 6 minutes

CHOCOLATE LOG:

Beat egg yolks with the sugar for 10 minutes. Add cocoa, sifted flour, and vanilla. Fold in egg whites beaten stiffly. Bake in a well-greased jelly roll pan at 450° for 6 minutes. Turn out on a floured kitchen towel and quickly roll up. When cooled, unroll enough to spread on the stiffly beaten whipped cream. Place roll on platter and ice.

CHOCOLATE LOG:

5 eggs, separated
2 cups confectioners' sugar
2 tablespoons cocoa
1 tablespoon flour, sifted
1 teaspoon vanilla
1 cup heavy cream, whipped and lightly sweetened

ICING:

Blend ingredients in blender until smooth; ice log.

ICING:

¼ pound butter, softened
1 2/3 cups confectioners' sugar
½ cup plus 2 tablespoons cocoa
½ cup heavy cream

"Log can be decorated with wavy fork lines or by spreading it to look like tree bark."
   Grace Barrington

GERMAN CHOCOLATE ANGEL PIE

Serves: 6-8
Preparation: 30 minutes (plus refrigeration)
Baking: 45-50 minutes for crust

CRUST:

Beat egg whites until they form peaks. Add salt and cream of tartar. Add sugar a little at a time. Fold in pecans and vanilla. Spread bottom and sides of a buttered 9-inch pie pan. Bake at 300° for 45 to 50 minutes until golden brown. Let cool.

CRUST:

2 egg whites
½ teaspoon salt
½ teaspoon cream of tartar
½ cup sugar
½ cup chopped pecans
½ teaspoon vanilla

FILLING:

Melt chocolate and water over low heat. Add vanilla and let cool completely. Whip cream and fold into chocolate. Spoon into pie crust. Chill.

FILLING:

4 ounces German sweet chocolate
3 tablespoons water
1 teaspoon vanilla
½ pint heavy cream

"Very rich."
   Miriam O'Neill

BROWNIE'S BROWNIES

Yield: 30-50 brownies
Preparation: 1 hour
Baking: 20-25 minutes

Melt butter and chocolate in a saucepan. Stir in the sugar and salt. Remove from heat. Beat in the eggs, one at a time, and stir in the flour, vanilla, and walnuts. Pour and scrape the mixture into a buttered 10 x 14-inch pan. Bake at 375° for 20 to 25 minutes. Cut while hot.

1 pound butter
4 squares unsweetened chocolate
2 cups sugar
1 teaspoon salt
4 eggs
1 cup flour
1 teaspoon vanilla
1 cup chopped walnuts

Carol Goble

BEV'S FOOL-PROOF FUDGE

Yield: Approximately 1½ pounds
Preparation: 5 minutes
Cooking: 15 minutes

In a large saucepan, mix sugar and cocoa well. Add milk and stir over medium heat to a rolling boil, stirring constantly. Cook approximately 10 minutes. Test a spoonful of chocolate mixture in a cup of cold water; when mixture forms a small ball remove from heat. Add vanilla, salt, butter, and peanut butter. Stir until smooth and creamy, about 3 minutes. Pour into a well-greased square dish. When completely cool, cut into squares.

2 cups sugar
2 heaping tablespoons cocoa
1 cup milk
1 teaspoon vanilla
Pinch of salt
½ stick butter
½ cup peanut butter
½ cup chopped nuts (optional)

Beverly Vermilyea

Copper chocolate pot, 1703

BITTER BRANDY

Serves: 4
Preparation: 10 minutes
(plus 24 hours refrigeration)

Melt chocolate in double boiler. Add brandy and salt. Mix thoroughly. Fold stiffly beaten whipped cream into mixture. Spoon into four compotes. Refrigerate for 24 hours.

Joanne Wylie

6 ounces semisweet chocolate
3 ounces brandy
¼ teaspoon salt
½ pint heavy cream

HEATH BAR DESSERT

Serves: 24
Preparation: 30-45 minutes
Baking: 1 hour (plus overnight refrigeration)

MERINGUES:
Whip egg whites until foamy. Add the sugar gradually and beat until very stiff. Line two 9 x 13-inch pans with foil and put half of this mixture in each. Bake at 300° for 1 hour. Cool. Run a spatula under the meringues to remove. Meringues will be hard and warped after cooking but soften after refrigeration. Place one of them on a large, flat tray or pan.

MERINGUES:
6 egg whites
1¾ cups sugar

FILLING:
Whip the cream and fold in coarsely crushed Heath Bars. Put half the filling on top of the first meringue; add the second meringue and top this with cream mixture. Decorate with chocolate shavings. Refrigerate immediately and leave overnight. Cut in squares to serve.

Mrs. A. Howard Stebbins III

FILLING:
1 pint whipping cream
12 Heath Bars
Chocolate shavings

Silver saucepan with wooden handle, 1759-80

Americans gained a reputation abroad for drinking in great quantities. Judging from the number of beverage recipes in eighteenth- and nineteenth-century cookbooks, one tends to conclude that the reputation was well deserved. Americans and Europeans alike, however, drank heartily because the quality of drinking water was not dependable. Cider and beer were the equivalents of today's sodas, consumed as thirst quenchers and with food. Spirits were also used as medicines and anesthetics. Many Americans began the day with a tumbler of rum or whiskey as an "eye-opener." Drinks were also regularly enjoyed in mid afternoon, at lunch and dinner, and as nightcaps to guard against chills. Despite the prevalence of liquor in colonial American life, society frowned upon over-indulgence and drunkenness.

"Cocktails" originally referred to a mixture of spirits, sugar, water, and bitters, but the "cocktail party" did not come into vogue until the twentieth century. Prior to this time, guests were always invited for dinner, not just drinks, and appetizers were rarely served. Many drink recipes developed in the eighteenth and nineteenth centuries, however, are quite appropriate for modern-day gatherings: punches, shrubs, flips, juleps, slings, and toddies.

Tea was also a standard beverage in early America. In fact, tea drinking was virtually a ritual. Hot tea was served in the morning, at four in the afternoon following the English custom, and to the ladies after dinner. Elaborate tea services were made of ceramics as well as silver. When English tea was banned during the Revolution, coffee became the patriotic substitute.

This brass coffee urn has an S-scroll handle and legs; it was probably made in England, 1725-75. The brass and steel coffee mill with wooden handle was made either in England or America, 1800-1825, while the cups and saucers in a grapeleaf pattern are Chinese export porcelain, 1790-1810.

ORANGE PUNCH

Yield: 25 servings
Preparation: 10 minutes

Make ice cubes with a cherry in each, or make 1 large ice block with cherries and mint leaves frozen in it. Thaw orange juice and lemonade in a punch bowl. Add bitter lemon and ginger ale. Float lemon and orange slices on top. Add ice. If desired, add bourbon to taste.

Maraschino cherries
Mint leaves
4 cans frozen orange juice, undiluted
2 cans frozen lemonade, undiluted
2 large bottles bitter lemon
2 28-ounce bottles ginger ale
Bourbon (optional)

Jackie Kelly

SPECIAL EGGNOG

Yield: Approximately 20 servings
Preparation: 30-40 minutes

Beat egg yolks until lemon in color. Add 2/3 cup sugar and beat well. Beat egg whites until stiff; add 1/3 cup sugar and beat well. Add softened ice cream to yolks; beat until most of the lumps are gone. Fold in egg whites and mix all ingredients. Serve in cups; sprinkle with nutmeg.

12 eggs, separated
1 cup superfine sugar
1 quart vanilla ice cream, softened
4 ounces light rum
4 ounces brandy
2 ounces bourbon
Nutmeg

Mrs. Charles G. Rivers, Jr.

WASSAIL BOWL PUNCH

Yield: Approximately 15 servings

Mix all ingredients over low heat. Serve hot.

1 quart tea
1 quart cranberry juice
1 quart apple juice
3 cinnamon sticks, 2 inches long each
12 whole cloves
1 cup sugar (less if frozen cranberry cocktail is used)
2 cups orange juice
¾ cup lemonade

Elizabeth Connell

CHAMPAGNE PUNCH

Yield: Approximately 30 servings
Preparation: 10 minutes (3 hours before serving)

Dissolve gelatin in 6 cups of boiling water. Add sugar and pineapple juice. Freeze in mold. Remove from freezer about 3 hours before using. Place in punch bowl and add the ginger ale and champagne to serve.

1 6-ounce package lime-flavored gelatin
2 cups sugar
2 46-ounce cans unsweetened pineapple juice
2 quarts ginger ale
1-1 ½ bottles champagne

"Lovely for a shower."
    Bobbie Longacre

LEMON PUNCH

Yield: 24 servings

Dissolve sugar in lemon juice. Add spirits and stir. To serve, place large block of ice in punch bowl. Pour in punch and soda water and stir. Garnish with thinly sliced lemons.

2 cups lemon juice
¾ cup sugar
1 quart Jamaican rum
1 pint brandy
1 cup apricot or peach brandy (or ½ cup apricot or peach liqueur)
1 quart soda water

Yuletide at Winterthur

PLANTER'S PUNCH

Yield: 1 serving

If fresh pineapple is used, muddle before adding other ingredients. Mix papaya juice, lime juice and rind, and rum together; shake well with cracked ice. Strain mixture into 12-ounce highball glass filled with cracked ice. Float cognac on top and decorate with oranges, pineapple, and cherries.

3 dashes pineapple juice or 4 slices fresh pineapple
½ ounce papaya juice
1 teaspoon lime juice and grated rind
1½ ounces rum
Cracked ice
1 teaspoon cognac
Slices of orange, pineapple and maraschino cherries

Winterthur Archives

JOAN'S BABY SHOWER PUNCH

Yield: 30 punch cup servings
Preparation: 1 ½ hours

In a large saucepan, bring to a boil water, sugar, cloves, cinnamon, allspice, ginger and rinds; reduce temperature and simmer 10 minutes. Let stand 1 hour. Add orange juice, lemon juice, and burgundy. Heat until steaming and serve from a large punch bowl.

1 quart water
3 cups sugar
12 whole cloves
1 4-inch stick cinnamon
6 whole allspice
½ teaspoon ground ginger
Rind of 1 orange
Rind of 1 lemon
2 cups orange juice
1 cup lemon juice
A fifth of burgundy

Lucie Frederick

CHRISTMAS PUNCH

Yield: Approximately 25 servings
Preparation: 10 minutes
(8 hours before serving)

Eight hours before serving, mix all ingredients. Just before serving, add ice.

1 46-ounce can unsweetened pineapple juice
1 46-ounce can unsweetened grapefruit juice
½ gallon cranberry juice
1 12-ounce can frozen orange juice, undiluted
1 28-ounce bottle lemon-lime soda
2 cups bourbon

Bobbie Longacre

WAGNER'S FISH HOUSE PUNCH

Yield: Approximately 50 servings

Mix all ingredients and pour over cracked ice.

1¾ pint lemon juice
3 pounds sugar
1 quart cognac brandy
1 pint peach brandy
1 pint Jamaican rum
4 quarts water
Cracked ice

Winterthur Archives 𝒲𝒜

SHERRY COBBLER

Yield: 1 serving

Fill a large tumbler halfway with crushed ice. Add fresh fruit, papaya juice, sherry, cherry brandy, and slice of orange.

Crushed ice
Fresh fruit, chopped small
1 teaspoon papaya juice
3 ounces dry sherry
3 ounces cherry brandy
1 slice orange

Winterthur Archives ℳ

HUGER EGGNOG

Yield: 12-15 servings
Preparation: 1 hour (begin day before serving)

One day before serving, separate eggs. Refrigerate whites in covered non-metal bowl. Beat yolks on medium high setting. Gradually add sugar until mixture is creamy yellow. Beat in bourbon. Place in another non-metal bowl and refrigerate to "cook" yolks (about 12 hours). Before serving, beat egg whites until stiff but not dry. Whip cream. Add brandy and rum to yolk mixture. Fold in egg whites and cream. Thin with milk and sprinkle with nutmeg, if desired. Serve with spoons rather than as liquid beverage.

12 eggs, separated
¾ cup sugar
6 ounces bourbon
1 quart whipping cream
6 ounces brandy
2 ounces dark Jamaican rum
Nutmeg (optional)

"From the nineteenth-century cookbook of the Huger house in Charleston, South Carolina. Traditionally served for annual New Year's Day open house."
Mrs. J. Ray Efird

DRUNKEN APRICOTS

Yield: 1 serving

Freeze apricots into ice cubes, chopping apricots into smaller pieces if necessary. Add Southern Comfort, filling the rest of wine glass with champagne. Add ice cube with apricot.

Apricots
1½ ounces Southern Comfort
Champagne
Ice cubes

Nancy Quaile

MINT JULEP

Yield: 1 serving

Place mint leaves in bottom of a glass and muddle thoroughly. With the back side of a tablespoon, press and wipe the crushed leaves round and round the glass all the way to the top to create the mint aroma. Pack each glass tightly with shaved ice. Pour in as much straight bourbon as the glass will hold. Add creme de menthe and insert a plastic straw down the side of the ice to the bottom of the glass. Garnish with sprig of mint. Sprinkle powdered sugar over top of sprig and ice. Place in refrigerator until glass is thoroughly frosted.

Winterthur Archives

30-40 separated mint leaves
Shaved ice
3 jiggers bourbon
1 teaspoon green creme de menthe
Sprig of mint
1 teaspoon powdered sugar

COFFEE SURPRISE

Yield: Approximately 50 servings

Mix all ingredients together and serve cold.

Winterthur Archives

2 gallons black coffee
1 quart strong cocoa made with milk
1 quart light cream
1 gallon coffee ice cream
1 fifth rum

UNION LEAGUE SPECIAL

Yield: 1 serving

Mix all ingredients together and serve in a small glass.

Winterthur Archives

¾ ounce orange juice
¾ ounce lemon juice
1 teaspoon sugar
Orange curacao
1-1½ ounces Jamaican rum
1½ jiggers rye whiskey

LUAU KIKI

Mix all juices together carefully, making sure cream of coconut is well blended. Add liqueur, wine, and rum to taste. Garnish with fruit and serve.

15 ounces cream of coconut
1 12-ounce can frozen pineapple juice, made according to directions
1 12-ounce can frozen pink lemonade, made according to directions
1 12-ounce can frozen orange juice, made according to directions
½ cup orange curacao or Cointreau
1 bottle white wine
2/3 bottle rum
Orange sections, shredded coconut, and cherries

Betty Betts

WINTERTHUR PUNCH

Yield: 12 servings

Pour all liquid ingredients into a bowl containing block of ice. Add garnishes.

1 quart sauterne
1 pint mineral water
12 ounces lemon juice
12 ounces cognac
6 ounces orange curacao
6 ounces grenadine
Block of ice
Slices of oranges, lemon and cherries
Bunch of green mint

Winterthur Archives 𝓜

COFFEE ROYALE

Yield: 30 servings

Freeze coffee into cubes. Just before serving, run the cubes through an ice crusher. Put all ingredients into a punch bowl; stir until most of the ice is melted and all is blended into a smooth, rich punch.

2 quarts coffee
½ cup rum (or more to taste)
2 quarts vanilla ice cream

"Excellent flavor; a nice change of pace from the usual party punch."
  Lucie Frederick

BRANDY COFFEE SUPREME

Yield: 1 serving

Rub rim of 10-ounce mug or cup with lemon peel. Add brandy and coffee. Add creme de cacao; top with whipped cream.

Strips of lemon peel
1½ ounces brandy
1 cup coffee
½ ounce creme de cacao
Whipped cream

Fay Gates

SCHLAG

For each serving, put into a mug a teaspoon of chocolate syrup and fill mug ¾ full with hot coffee. Add a scoop of vanilla ice cream or a generous serving of whipped cream. Top with a jigger of creme de menthe. Serve at once.

Chocolate syrup
Double-strength coffee
Vanilla ice cream or whipped cream
Creme de menthe

"Coffee and dessert in one; a light way to end an elegant meal."
  Mrs. Charles G. Rivers, Jr.

Tin-glazed earthenware punch bowl, 1732

WINTERTHUR ICED TEA

Yield: 10-15 servings

Add maple syrup to tea while it is hot. Let stand until cool. Put in refrigerator until thoroughly cold. Add ice and lemon juice; slices of lemon may also be added. Put mint sprig at top of each glass.

Winterthur Archives ℳ

1 gallon of tea, not too strong
4 ounces maple syrup
Ice
2 ounces lemon juice
Slices of lemon (optional)
Sprigs of mint

FRUITED ICED TEA

Yield: 8-10 servings

Boil the 2 cups of water and sugar for 5 minutes. Add orange juice, lemon juice, tea, and 2 quarts of cold water. Add ice and serve.

Bobbie Longacre

2 cups water
1½ cups sugar
2 cups orange juice
¾ cup lemon juice
1 quart strong tea (10-12 tea bags per quart of water)
2 quarts cold water

HOT COCOA MIX

Yield: 20 servings
Preparation: 5 minutes

Mix all ingredients. Store in an airtight container. For each serving, use 1/4 to 1/3 cup of mix for each cup of hot water. Stir well. Can be stored for several months.

Dorothy J. Hough

4 cups powdered nonfat dry milk
½ cup cocoa
½ teaspoon salt
1 cup sugar
1 cup nondairy creamer

STANDARD EQUIVALENTS

Pinch or dash = less than ⅛ teaspoon
3 teaspoons = 1 tablespoon = ½ fluid ounce
2 tablespoons = 1 fluid ounce
4 tablespoons = ¼ cup = 2 fluid ounces
5 1/3 tablespoons = 1/3 cup = 2 2/3 fluid ounces
8 tablespoons = ½ cup = 4 fluid ounces
12 tablespoons = ¾ cup = 6 fluid ounces
16 tablespoons = 1 cup = 8 ounces

2 cups = 1 pint = 16 fluid ounces
4 cups = 1 quart
2 pints = 1 quart
4 quarts = 1 gallon
11 quarts = 1 peck
4 pecks = 1 bushel
16 ounces = 1 pound

SUBSTITUTIONS

Baking powder	1 teaspoon	= 1/4 teaspoon baking soda plus ⅝ teaspoon cream of tartar
double acting	1 teaspoon	= 1½ teaspoons phosphate or tartrate baking powder
Chocolate, sweetened	1 ounce	= 1 square
unsweetened	1 ounce	= 3 tablespoons cocoa, plus 1 tablespoon butter or fat
semisweet	1 2/3 ounce	= 1 ounce unsweetened plus 4 teaspoons sugar
Cocoa	1 pound	= 4 cups
	3 tablespoons plus 1 tablespoon fat	= 1 ounce unsweetened chocolate
Cornstarch	1 tablespoon	= 2 tablespoons flour or 1½ teaspoons arrowroot
Cream, heavy	1 cup	= 2 cups whipped
Flour, cake	1 cup sifted	= ⅞ cup sifted all-purpose flour, or 1 cup less 2 tablespoons
Garlic	1 small clove	= ⅛ teaspoon powder
Ginger	1 teaspoon grated	= ¼ teaspoon ground
Herbs, fresh chopped	1 tablespoon	= 1 teaspoon dried
Ketchup	½ cup	= ½ cup tomato sauce plus 1 tablespoon vinegar, 2 tablespoons sugar, and ⅛ teaspoon cloves

Continued

SUBSTITUTIONS

Lemon	1	=	2 to 3 tablespoons juice
Milk, whole	1 cup	=	¼ dry whole milk plus ⅞ cup water
skim	1 cup	=	1/3 cup instant nonfat dry milk plus ¾ cup water
soured	1 cup	=	1 tablespoon vinegar plus whole milk to make one cup (let stand 5 minutes)
Mustard	1 teaspoon dry	=	1 tablespoon prepared
Onion	½ cup fresh chopped	=	2 tablespoons dry minced
Orange	1 medium-sized	=	6 to 8 tablespoons juice
Orange rind, grated	1 medium-sized	=	2 to 3 tablespoons
Parsley	Any quantity parsley	=	Equal quantity celery leaves
Potatoes	1 pound or 3 medium-sized	=	2½ cups, cooked
Rice, regular	1 pound or 2 cups, uncooked	=	6 cups, cooked
wild	1 pound or 2 cups, uncooked	=	8 cups, cooked
Sour cream	1 cup	=	1 cup evaporated milk plus 1 tablespoon vinegar or 1 cup cottage cheese blended with 2 tablespoons milk and 1 tablespoon lemon juice
Sugar, granulated	1 pound	=	2 cups
brown, packed	1 pound	=	2¼ cups
confectioners'	1 pound	=	3½ to 4 cups
confectioners'	1¾ cups	=	1 cup granulated sugar
non calorie sweetener	⅛ teaspoon	=	1 teaspoon sugar
Tapioca, for thickening	1 tablespoon quick-cooking	=	1 tablespoon flour
Tea	1 pound	=	125 cups
Tomato juice	1 cup	=	½ cup tomato sauce plus ½ cup water
Tomato sauce	2 cups	=	¾ cup tomato paste plus 1 cup water
Yeast, compressed	1 cake (3/5 ounce)	=	1 package active dry yeast
active dry	1 package	=	1 tablespoon
Yogurt	1 cup	=	1 cup buttermilk

INDEX

ORDER FORM

Winterthur's Culinary Collection may be purchased at the Winterthur Bookstore or may be ordered by mail. Please make checks payable to WINTERTHUR MUSEUM and send to:

Winterthur Bookstore/WCC
Winterthur Museum and Gardens
Winterthur, Delaware 19735

Please send _____ copies of **Winterthur's Culinary Collection.** A check for $12.95 plus $1.50 for postage and handling per book is enclosed.

NAME _____

ADDRESS _____

CITY _____ STATE_____

ZIP CODE _____

ORDER FORM

Winterthur's Culinary Collection may be purchased at the Winterthur Bookstore or may be ordered by mail. Please make checks payable to WINTERTHUR MUSEUM and send to:

Winterthur Bookstore/WCC
Winterthur Museum and Gardens
Winterthur, Delaware 19735

Please send _____ copies of **Winterthur's Culinary Collection.** A check for $12.95 plus $1.50 for postage and handling per book is enclosed.

NAME _____

ADDRESS _____

CITY _____ STATE_____

ZIP CODE _____

ORDER FORM

Winterthur's Culinary Collection may be purchased at the Winterthur Bookstore or may be ordered by mail. Please make checks payable to WINTERTHUR MUSEUM and send to:

Winterthur Bookstore/WCC
Winterthur Museum and Gardens
Winterthur, Delaware 19735

Please send _____ copies of **Winterthur's Culinary Collection.** A check for $12.95 plus $1.50 for postage and handling per book is enclosed.

NAME _____

ADDRESS _____

CITY _____ STATE_____

ZIP CODE _____